AISLIN 10
MONTRÉAL
THE GAZETTE

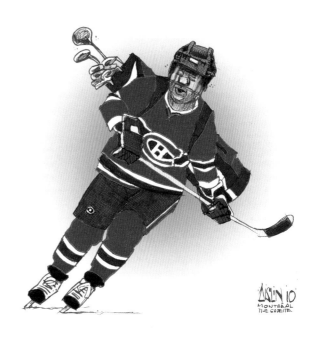

This book is dedicated to…

Special thanks as always to Mary, and with appreciation to Christian Vachon.

Was It Good For You?

...and other recent cartoons by

With an introduction by Rick Mercer

Text by Terry Mosher

Bibliothèque - Library
BEACONSFIELD
303 boul. Beaconsfield,
Beaconsfield Qc H9W 4A7

www.lindaleith.com

LINDA LEITH PUBLISHING

Library and Archives Canada Cataloguing in Publication

Aislin
    Was it good for you? : and other recent cartoons / by Aislin.

Issued also in electronic format.
ISBN 978-0-9878317-6-7

    1. Canada--Politics and government--2006- --Caricatures
and cartoons. 2. Canadian wit and humor, Pictorial. I. Title.

NC1449.A37A4 2012   971.07'30207   C2012-902132-6

Cover illustration by AISLIN
Layout, design and electronic imaging by Mary Hughson
Printed and bound in Canada by Marquis Imprimeur inc.

Dépôt légal: 3e trimestre 2012
Bibliothèque nationale du Québec and National Library of Canada.

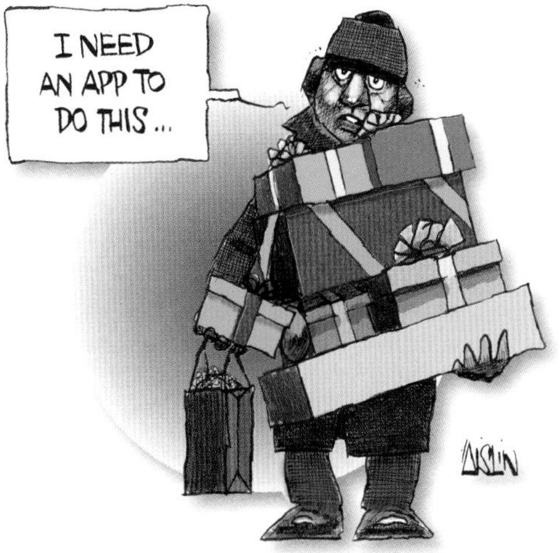
I NEED AN APP TO DO THIS...
AISLIN

OUR PICK? GOVERNOR GENERAL RICK MERCER...

AISLIN 10
MONTREAL
THE GAZETTE

Introduction

The name Aislin is derived from a Gaelic word meaning "dream,"
but to many of the more dubious members of Canada's political class,
Aislin is something more of a nightmare. It's a name that has become
synonymous with biting political satire and razor-sharp wit.
But more importantly he is Canada's most celebrated shit disturber.
I admire that more than you can imagine.

In the age of Twitter when most of us are trying desperately
to inject 140-character messages with humour, charm, or wit,
Aislin uses far fewer words and always conveys so much more.
Throughout his four decade-long career, Aislin's pen has relentlessly
attacked the pomposity and arrogance that has far too often poisoned the
public debate in Canada. The cartoons are funny because they are true.

Was It Good For You? is a piercing collection of the best of
Aislin's recent work. I can honestly answer the question posed by the
book's title with a resounding "Yes." Some of the individuals found within
this collection might disagree.

Rick Mercer

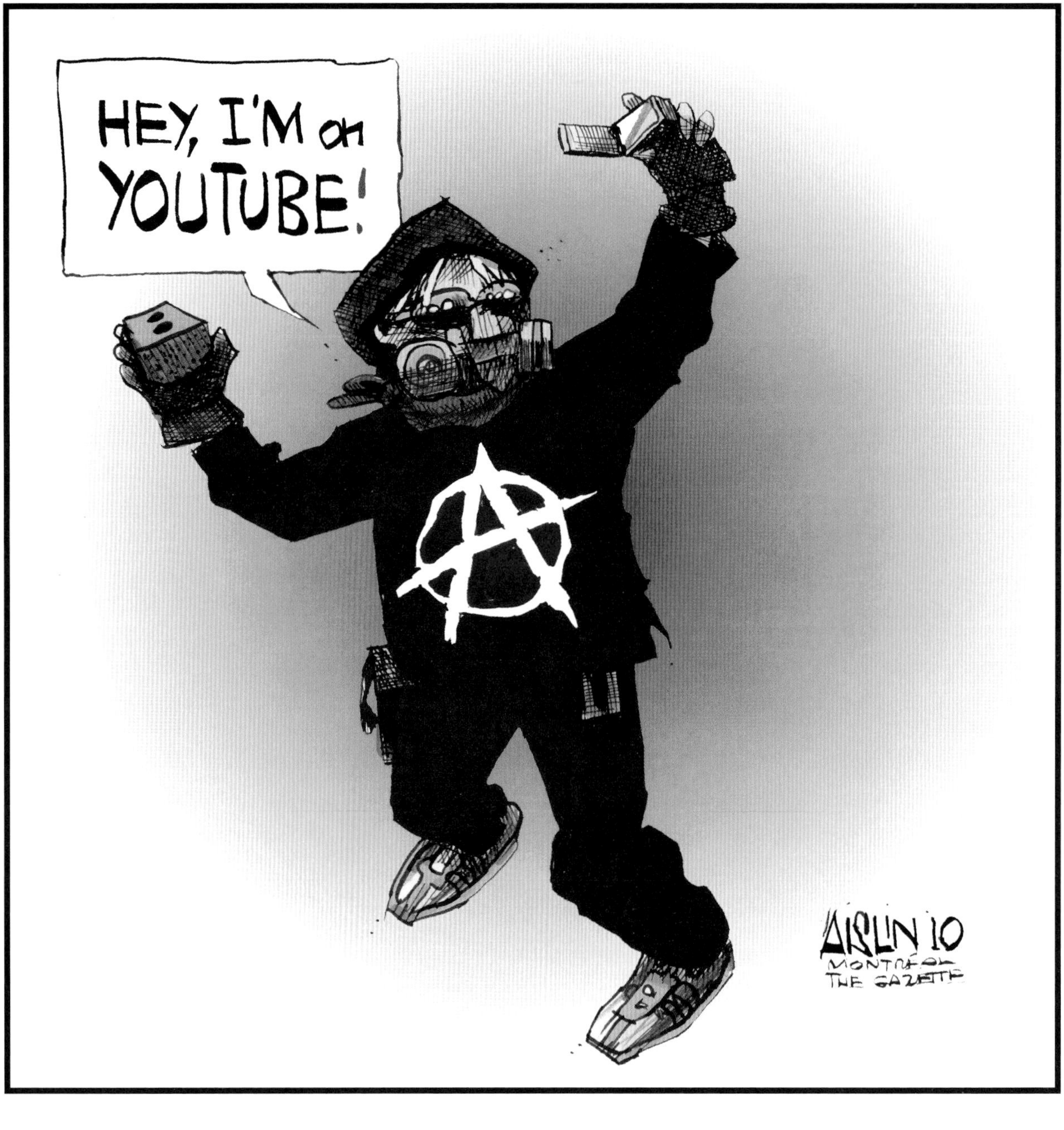
HEY, I'M on YOUTUBE!
AISLIN 10
MONTREAL THE GAZETTE

We're Angry

While choosing the cartoons to be included in this book – all favourites that I have drawn over the past three years – I was struck by how many of these sketches reflect how angry we have become these days; well 99% of us, anyway. We are even angry with those who are attempting to demonstrate our anger! The reason for this outrage is quite obvious in some cases. With 1% of our population earning 25% of our collective income, the OCCUPY WALL STREET movement and its offshoots made perfect sense. But there would also seem to be a trickle-down anger with the clogging of our public systems and so many other aspects of our daily lives.

The OCCUPY WALL STREET movement spread to Canada…

…even if over 99% of the 99% chose not to participate in the public protests.

Montreal seemed more ready than most cities to express its outrage…

…as it subsequently demonstrated in student demos over an increase in tuition fees.

CURRENT MONTREAL FASHION STATEMENTS

Wear a RED patch if you support the demonstrators...

Wear a GREEN patch if you think they all should be in school...

Wear a WHITE patch if you would like to see an armistice...

Wear a BROWN patch if you think it's all so much bull***t...

"AISLIN 12"
MONTREAL
THE GAZETTE

Montrealers took to wearing coloured patches to show their allegiances…

…while tourists were urged to fit right in.

Some youths were innocently caught up in the process…

… while several student leaders seemed intent on making a name for themselves.

There was a time when youthful protest was based on a love of mankind.

The motivation for protest would seem to be quite different today.

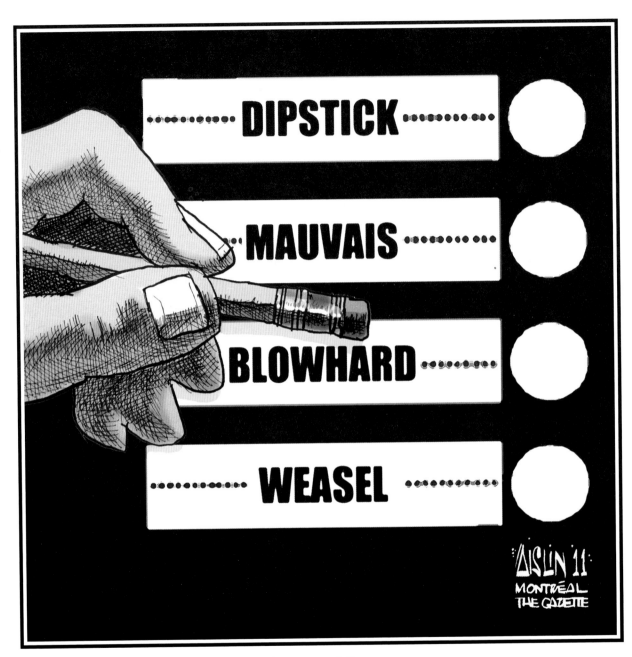

We're angry at the numbskull individuals we voted for…

…and we're fed up with endless government inquiries and the studies that they create.

We're suspicious of any and all industrial initiatives.

'GREENWASHING' ALL TOO COMMON

A new study has found that nearly all "green" consumer products make a false, misleading or unproven environmental claim to attract eco-conscious shoppers…

And we inherently know that advertisers habitually lie to us.

Most of us resent security cameras being posted absolutely everywhere…

…while there seems to be no escape from ubiquitous technologies.

We hate those intrusive security searches at all of our airports…

…almost as much as those who have to search us hate having to do so!

We pine away for our balmy winters during our now brutally hot summers…

And, all winter, we daydream about pleasant summertime activities.

We hate graffiti almost as much as we hate…

…having to exercise to only delay the inevitable.

If we're smart, we'll do anything to avoid a visit to the hospital…

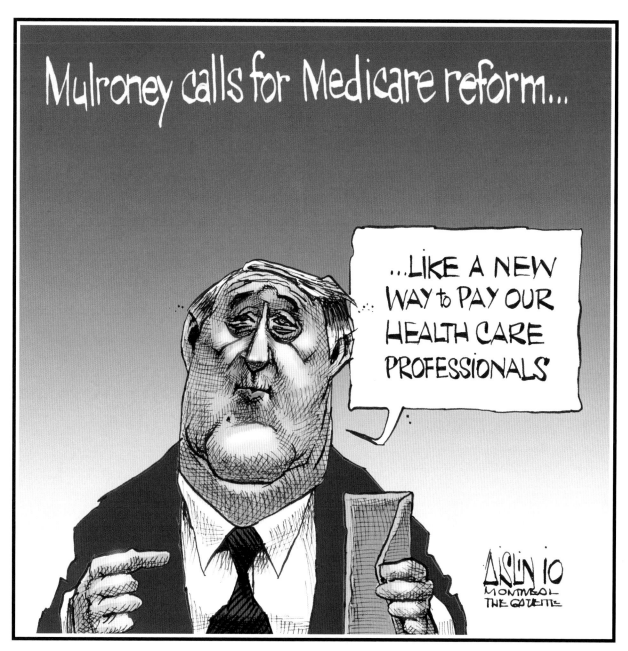

…and we're fed up to the teeth with opinions on Medicare.

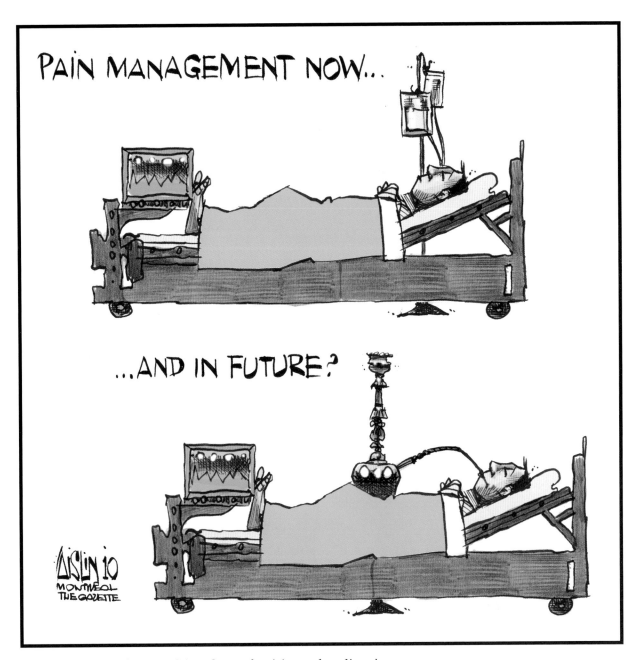

We've spent too long waiting for authorities to legalize drugs…

A solution..?

CONDOS

…and a majority of us want nothing to do anymore with organized religion. Above is my suggestion as to what should be done with St. Peter's in Rome.

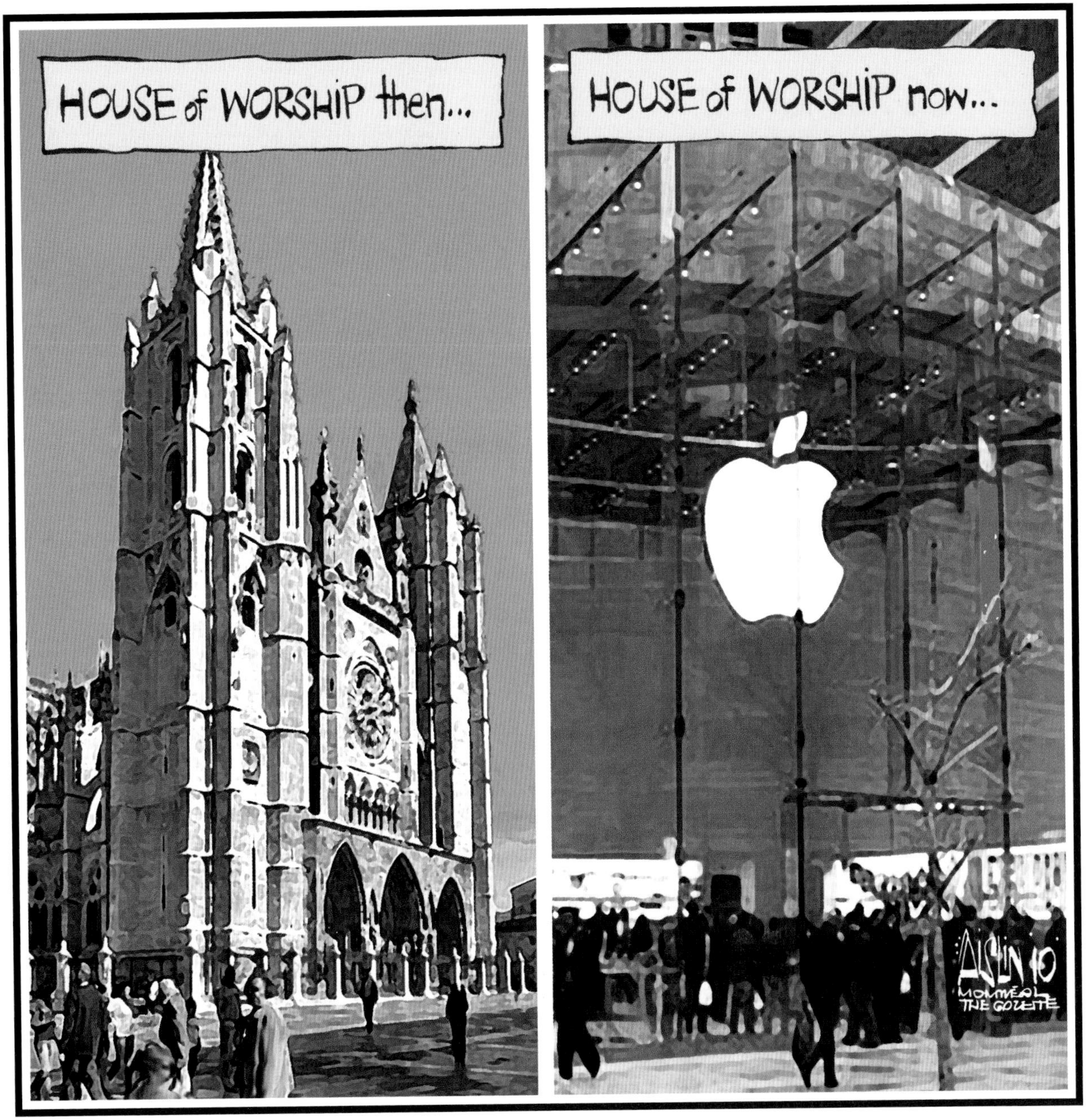
HOUSE of WORSHIP then...
HOUSE of WORSHIP now...

We're All Technobubbled!

The new cathedrals would appear to be Apple stores – while Steve Jobs has become a contemporary Jesus figure. Indeed, after Jobs died, I used the cartoon above as my personal screen saver. I'm as hooked on technology as anyone else, given that I use a MacBook Air, an iPhone and an iPad on a daily basis. Several older iPods and Powerbooks have now been consigned to the used stuff drawer along with all those sets of (useless) ear buds. Curiously, I've never ever used a PC or a Blackberry. I wouldn't know how. Nevertheless, the worrisome aspect of technology is that it will be eliminating a great number of things in my life that I will miss dearly.

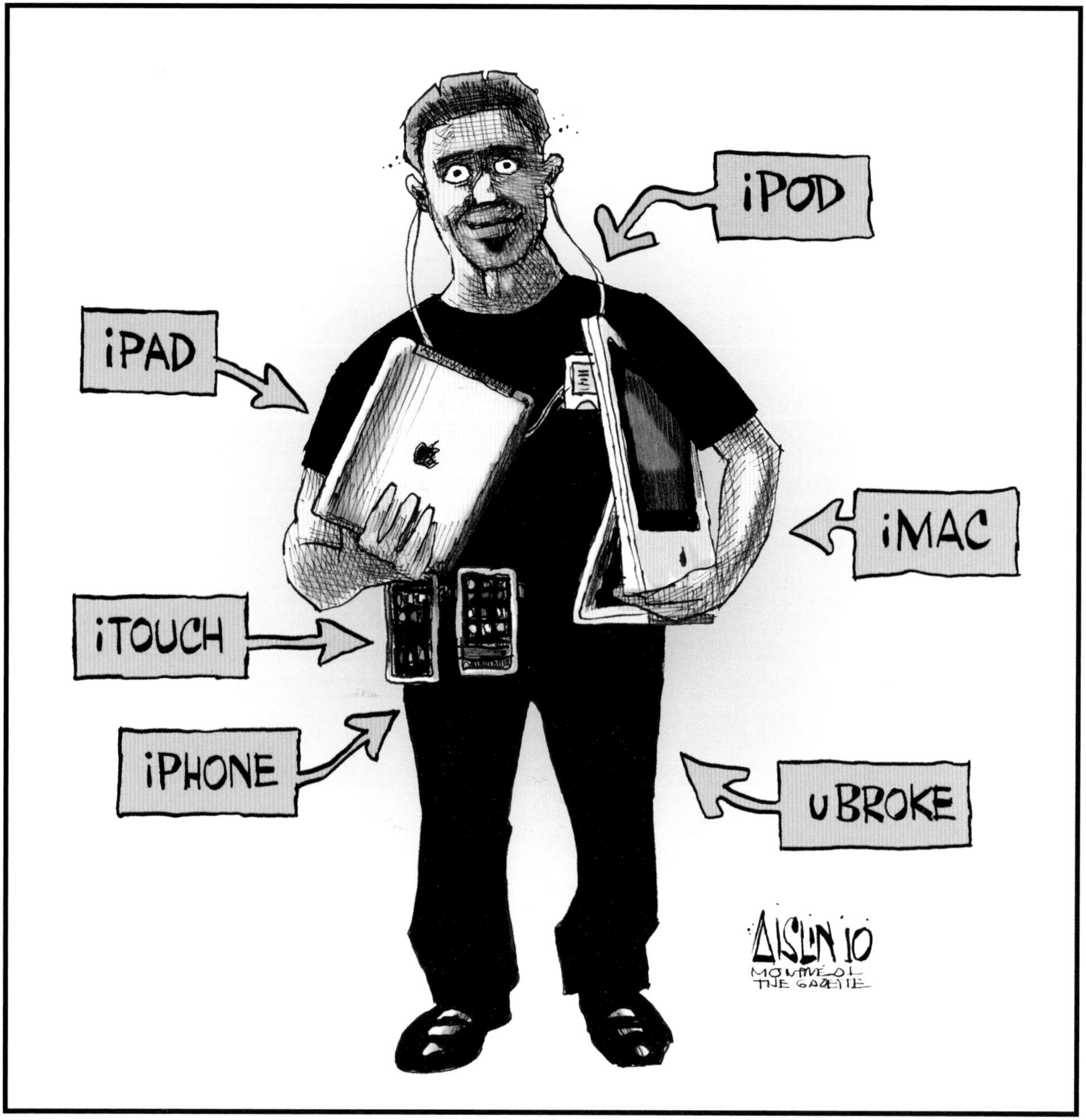
iPOD
iPAD
iMAC
iTOUCH
iPHONE
uBROKE
AISLIN '10
MONTREAL
THE GAZETTE

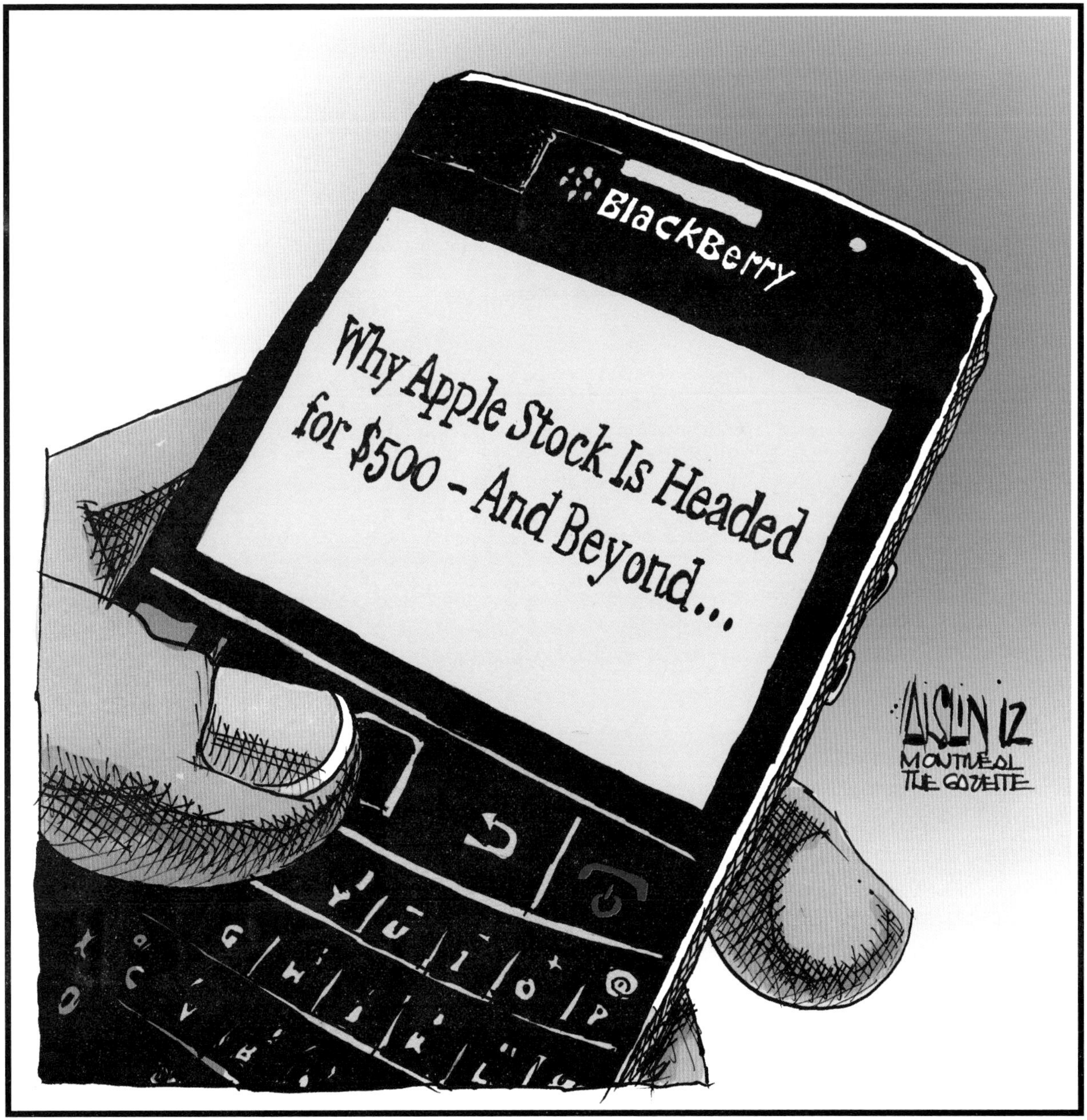
BlackBerry
Why Apple Stock Is Headed for $500 – And Beyond...
AISLIN 12
MONTREAL THE GAZETTE

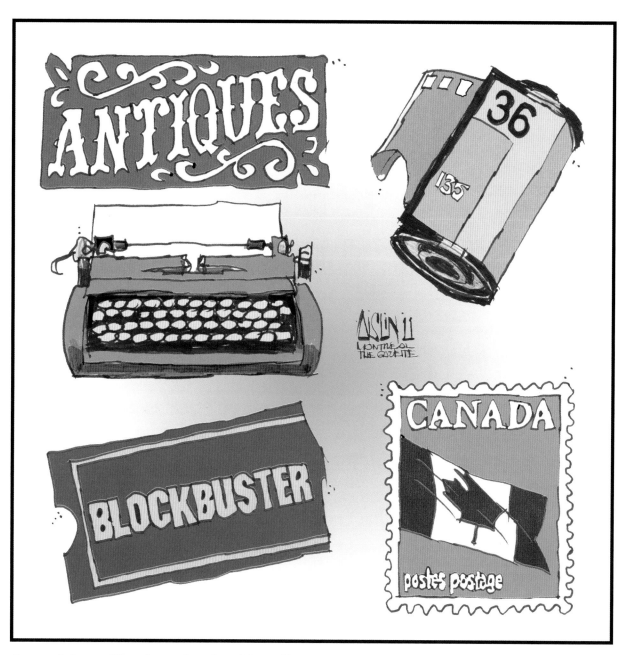

Some of the stuff we have already said goodbye to.

What with email, hardly anyone even noticed a recent postal strike.

Real journalism is losing its way…

…while printed newspapers appear to be a thing of the past.

It's becoming harder to find an actual book in a bookstore…

…not that we would mind if some of them were to disappear.

Does this mean the eventual disappearance of libraries…

...and any kind of record of the important things worth remembering?

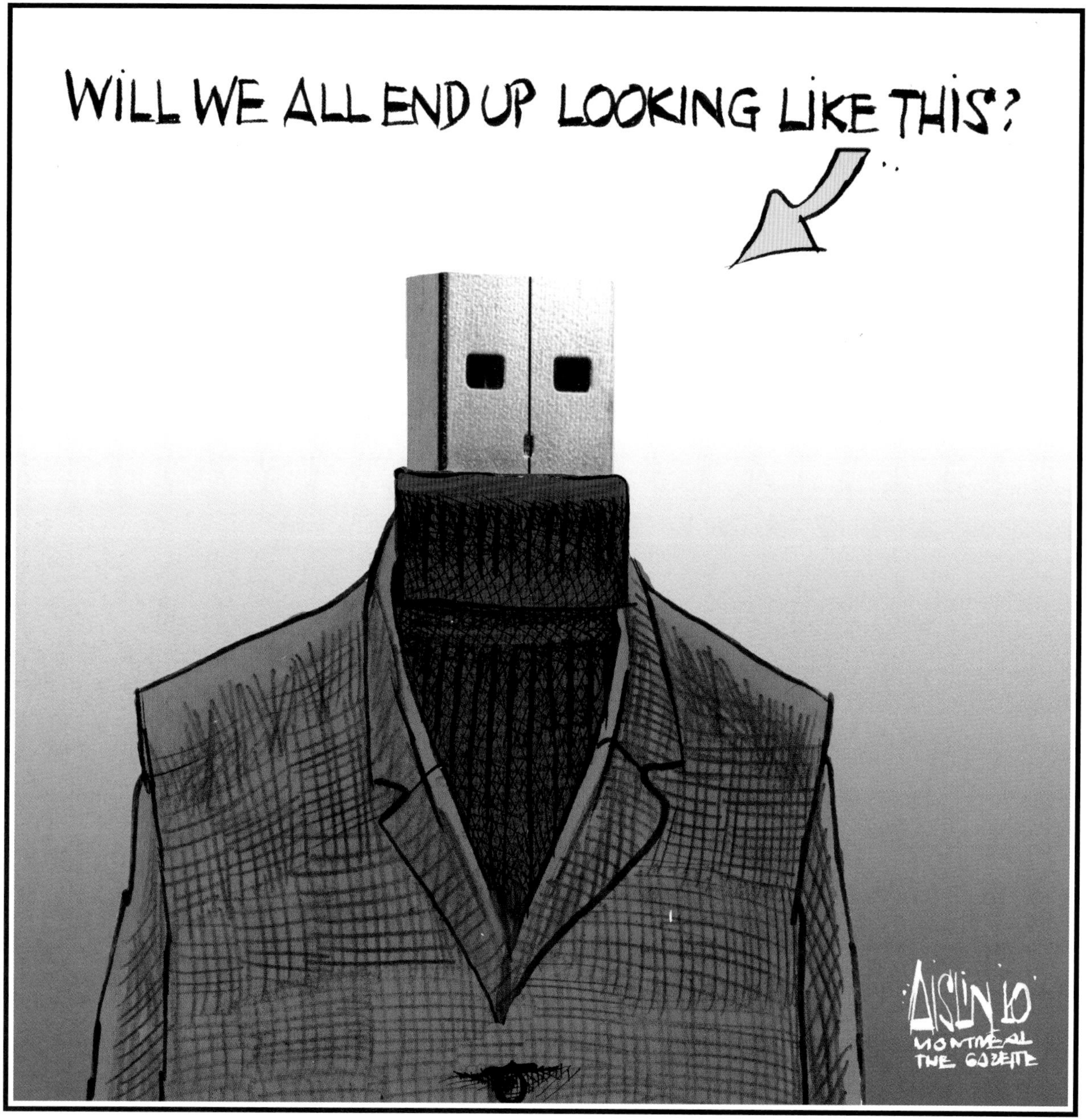
WILL WE ALL END UP LOOKING LIKE THIS?
AISLIN 10
MONTREAL THE GAZETTE

Google seeks to know what you want before you do

Ever wish you could type a few letters into Google and the search engine wou[ld kn]ow what you we[nt ... A]nd now it does. Meet Goo[gle t]he latest in a l[...] [b]y the world's larg[...] [to] bring big[...]ter results to its [...] users.

THERE'S NO GOD ....ONLY GOOGLE

AISLIN 10
MONTREAL
THE GAZETTE

Worrisome, isn't it? So, to find the answer to all these concerns, why don't we simply ask Google?

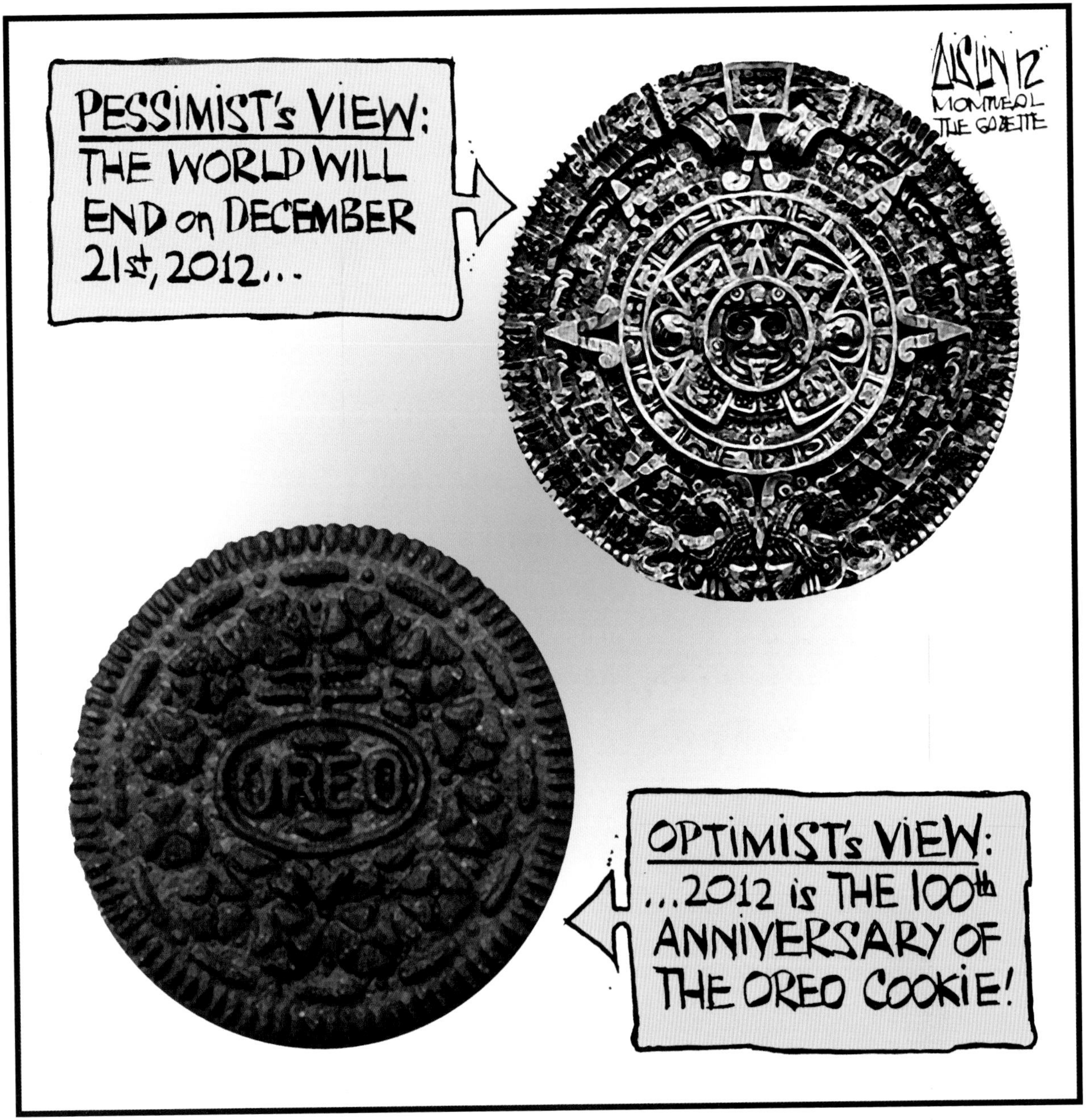
PESSIMIST's VIEW:
THE WORLD WILL END on DECEMBER 21st, 2012...
AISLIN 12
MONTREAL THE GAZETTE
OREO
OPTIMIST's VIEW:
...2012 is THE 100th ANNIVERSARY OF THE OREO COOKIE!

Will the World Ending in December Save Us All From Christmas Shopping?

A Mayan calendar has predicted that the world will end on December 21, 2012. The doomsday hype around this prediction has blossomed into a major new presence on the Internet. Optimists, on the other hand, have turned towards the celebration of the 100th anniversary of the Oreo cookie. Barack Obama strikes us as being quite the optimist given what he has to put up with – like Republicans and the medical lobby. Obama also gets our vote for having rid the world of Osama bin Laden, never mind slowly extracting the West from futile wars in both Iraq and Afghanistan. Nevertheless, the tensions of the world won't be disappearing any time soon, given the number of other troubling spots on the horizon.

A burning hot August in Washington – and we don't mean the weather.

Obama's attempt at establishing health care in America

Tea Party leader arrested on gun charges

American Thanksgiving

Quite an accomplishment!

Osama bin Laden is no more.

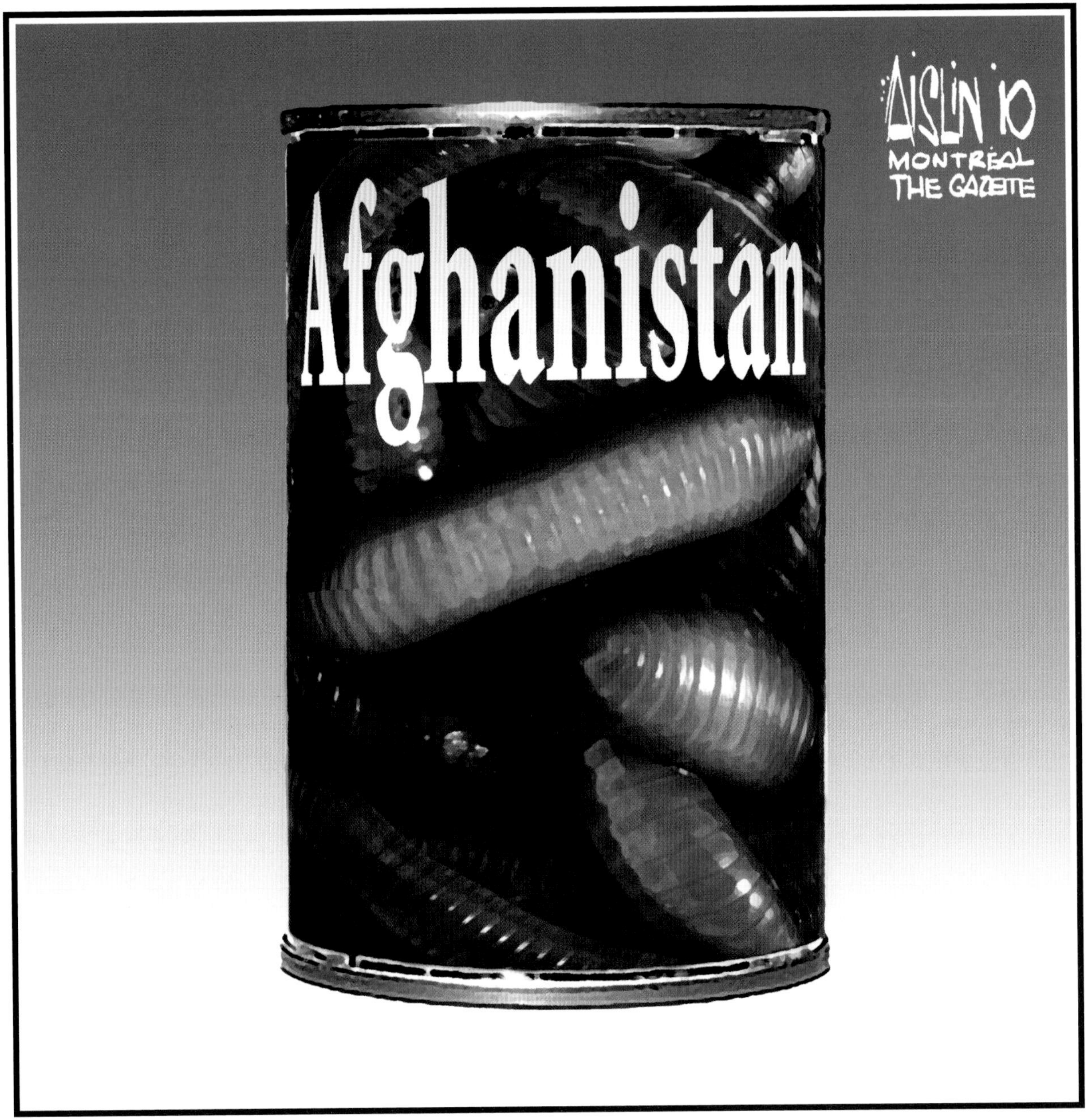
Afghanistan
AISLIN 10
MONTREAL
THE GAZETTE

Afghan President Hamid Karzai threatens to join the Taliban.

A purple finger is proof of having voted (once) in an Afghani election.

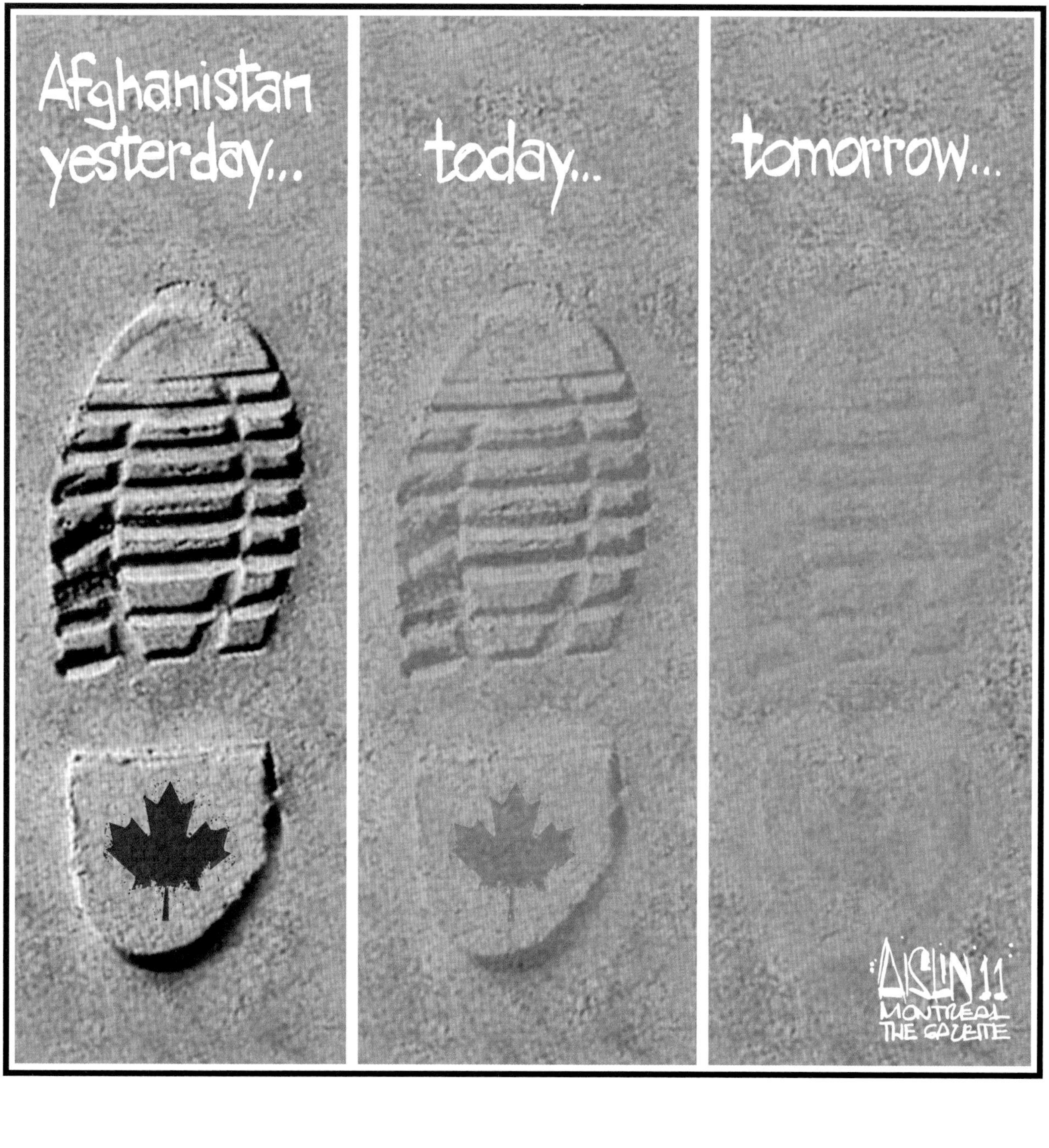
Afghanistan yesterday...
today...
tomorrow...
AISLIN 11
MONTREAL THE GAZETTE

As our troops begin to vacate Afghanistan…

...concerns are expressed for Canadian interests in Libya.

If nothing else, the Arab Spring sure is loud.

Paranoid concerns are expressed about a mosque located close to the site of 09/11.

Most powerfully recorded earthquake and tsunami hit Japan…with apologies to Hokusai.

Greece becomes the most financially unstable country in Europe.

President of Syria, Bashar Hafez al-Assad

Youngster Kim Jong-un is the third Kim to rule North Korea

And then there is eternally conflicted Pakistan

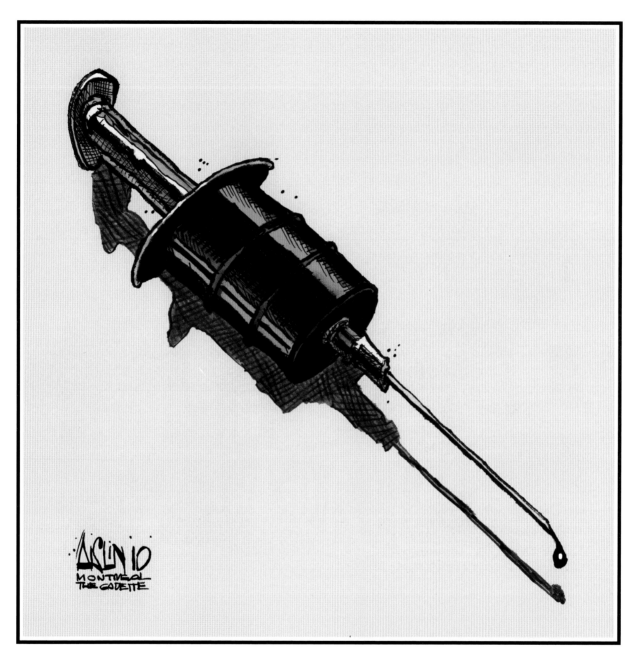

Most of our problems today come from the world being addicted to oil

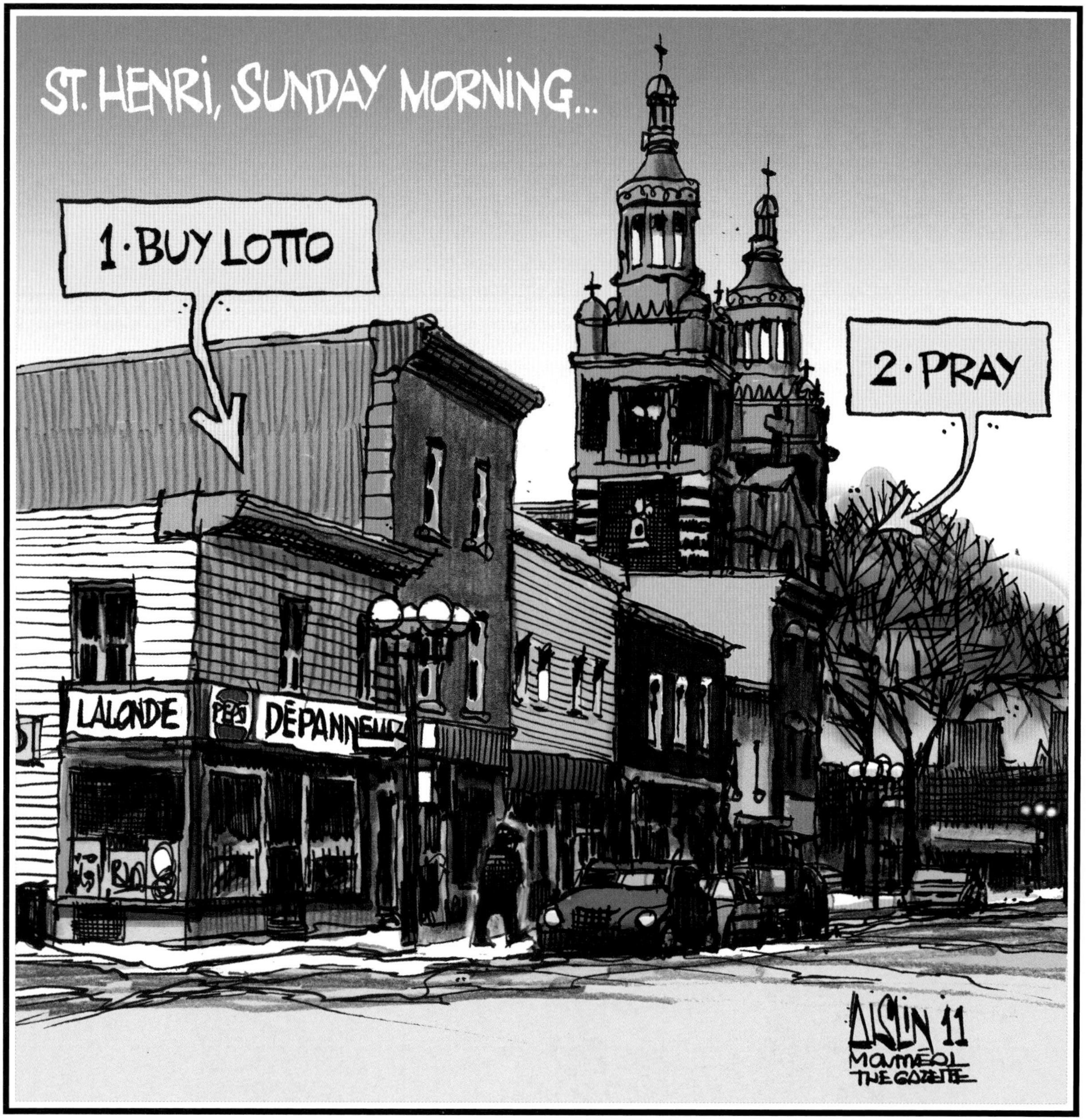
ST. HENRI, SUNDAY MORNING...
1·BUY LOTTO
2·PRAY
LALONDE
AISLIN 11
MONTREAL
THE GAZETTE

The scariest thing I saw this week: A woman riding a bike – while texting...

STREET SKETCH

AISLIN 11
MONTREAL
THE GAZETTE

A Sketchbook in Hand

I'm a big believer in surprising readers with a variety of techniques to keep them interested – and hopefully coming back for more. Often, a simple sketch of a local street scene, a favourite neighbourhood locale or even a drawing created while touring elsewhere can be turned into a political cartoon. I simply add a voice balloon to the initial sketch, commenting on a topic of the day. A good example of this was a sketch I did of the Battery neighbourhood from a distance while visiting St. John's, Newfoundland. Shortly after that, there was a rumour that Muammar Gaddafi might be stopping over for a brief stay in St. John's. How bizarre would that have been? So I simply added a Bedouin tent (with camel) hanging off the side of Signal Hill to the original sketch.

Rumours of illicit spying taking place at Montreal's city hall

Schwartz's delicatessen will be bought by a group that includes Céline Dion's husband.

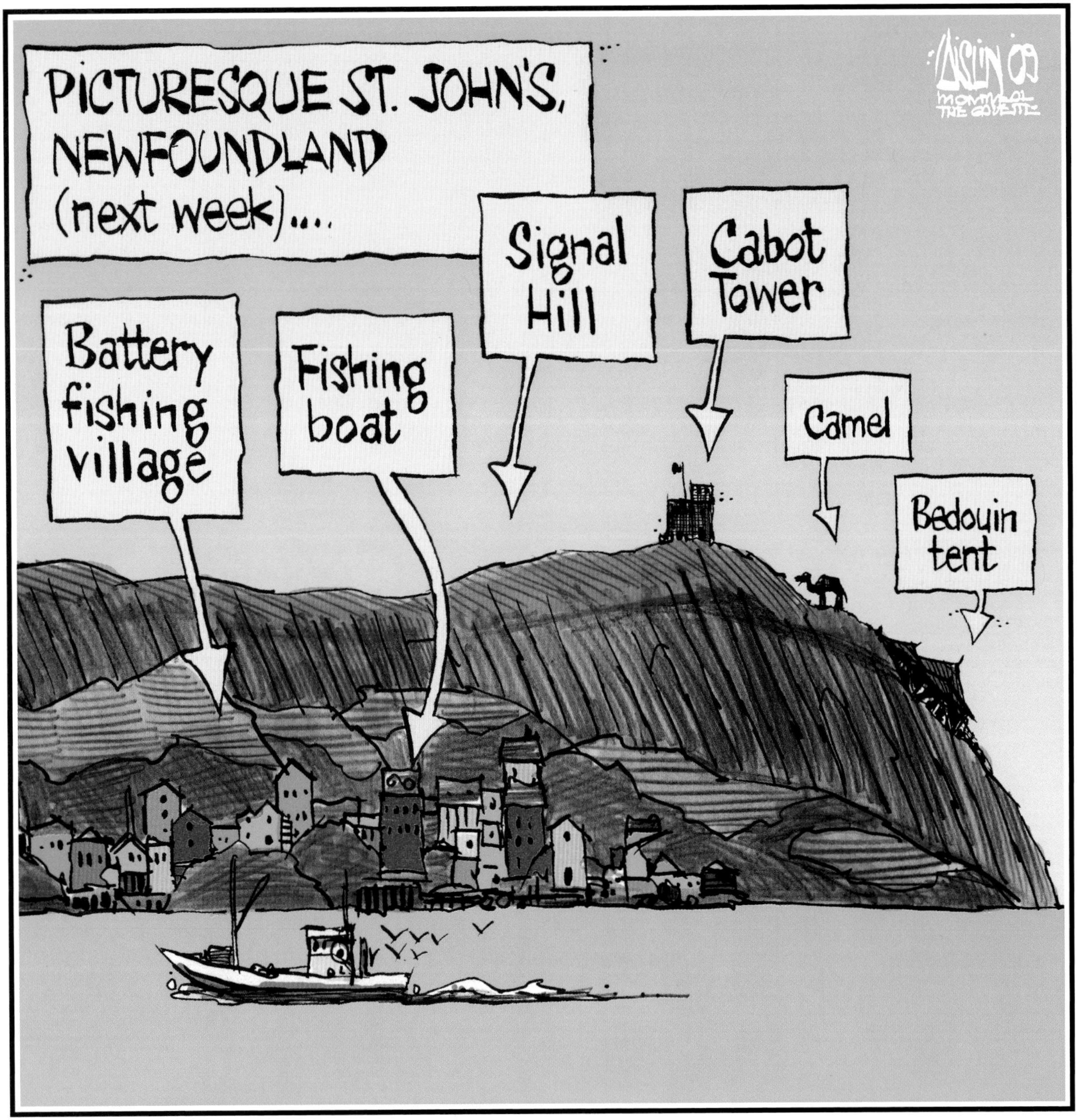
PICTURESQUE ST. JOHN'S, NEWFOUNDLAND (next week)....
Battery fishing village
Fishing boat
Signal Hill
Cabot Tower
Camel
Bedouin tent

A visit to my favourite library

Hanging out at Montreal's bus station

A sketch of two Montreal street characters during a July heat wave

An Image for Canada

The United States, of course, has the bald eagle – and McDonalds. Canada has the beaver and – Tim Hortons? Frankly, after having drawn hundreds of diligent, self-effacing beavers, I'm fed up with this glorified rodent as a visual symbol for Canada. Why not adopt the high-flying Canada Goose instead? These ubiquitous geese fly at great heights signaling our dramatic change in seasons during migration periods. Furthermore, their appearance is far more dramatic than that of snowbirds. And, speaking of that, this corner particularly likes the fact that the Canada goose is now famous for taking gigantic dumps all over America.

Australia displaces Canada at the number one position in a quality-of-life survey

Will America declare an additional war on our Canada goose?

Moose antlers, a Canada goose head, a polar bear body, a beaver tail, hockey gauntlets, and a double-double thrown in for good measure.

The Republicans have an elephant and the Democrats a donkey. What animals should represent Canada's political parties? You sent us 214 suggestions. For the Bloc Québécois, three Gazette readers thought of the skunk. But the winner was David Fletcher who specifically suggested PEPE LE PEW...

...the stereotypical French skunk with the malodorous scent who just can't take "Non" for an answer. Tomorrow: The Green Party

We received forty-two suggestions for an animal to represent the Liberal Party of Canada, with three of those readers — Glenn Bradley, Milda Weiss and Leo Schryburt — choosing the moose..... Perfect!

YOUR SUGGESTIONS FOR A REPRESENTATIVE ANIMAL FOR THE GREEN PARTY:

Dodo bird (twice), black-tailed prairie dog, kiwi bird, sloth (twice), the beaver (twice), gorilla, Piglet, March Hare, polar bear, rabbit (twice), giraffe, albatross, unicorn, chameleon, white owl, cow, turtle, raccoon, hedgehog, the bee, gecko, mouse, cricket, cuckoo bird, Bigfoot, turtle, loon and, our favourite, from Gazette reader Joan Parker, the green parrot (given that it keeps repeating the same words over and over again)...

POLLY WANT a SUSTAINABLE ECOSYSTEM!

And an animal for the NDP? Reader Betty Stockton has suggested the chameleon with its highly developed ability to change colour...

Gazette readers were asked to send in animal symbols for Canadian political parties.

Eight-year-old Ethan Grace has suggested the weasel as being the perfect symbol for the Conservatives...

...and all the other Canadian political parties!

Will our majestic northern lights soon be outshone?

America holds up the construction of TransCanada's Keystone pipeline

When we think of Alberta, we think of oil as its symbol

Things are changing dramatically in Canada: Toronto chose a redneck mayor, while Calgarians elected a progressive Muslim.

Conrad Black is sent back to a Florida jail.

Is the pompous, vainglorious Conrad Black actually the perfect symbol for the fading Toronto Establishment?

Stephen Harper has his majority

PANHANDLER OUTSIDE of EAST BLOCK

The Ottawa Blues

Here's a good Canadian trivia question for you: Can you name the five Leaders of the Opposition that Prime Minister Stephen Harper has faced in Ottawa's House of Commons over the past six years? There's no question that Harper is very good at chewing up and spitting out the Opposition. In fact, the three leaders of the major political parties that faced Harper in the May 2nd, 2012

federal election are all gone. Granted, our greatest loss was NDP leader Jack Layton, who died of cancer shortly after the election. The NDP had accomplished the unheard-of feat of taking a majority of seats in Quebec. But, when all was said and done, Harper had his majority, allowing him to get on with the business of changing Ottawa into a far more conservative and nasty place.

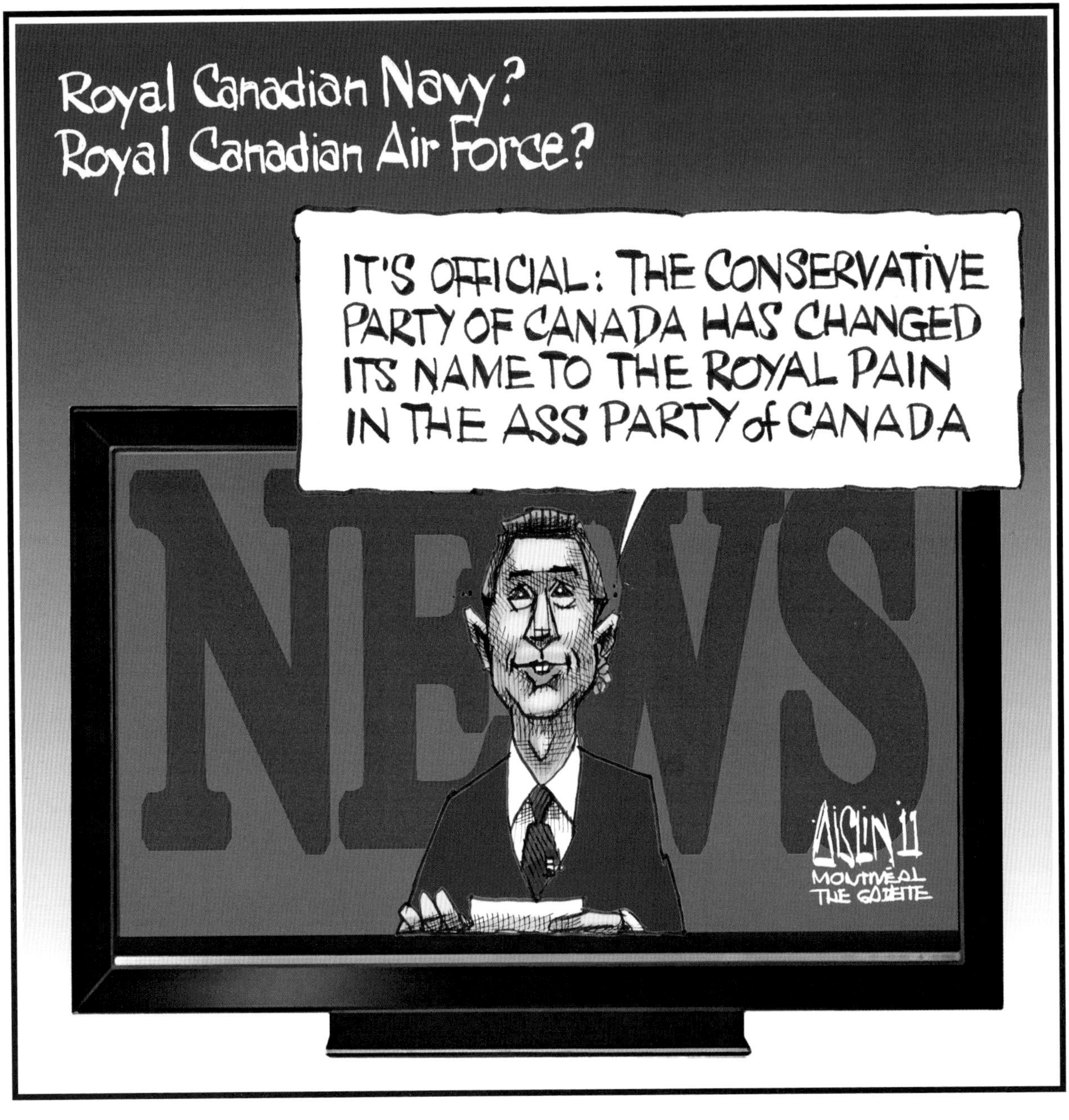
Royal Canadian Navy?
Royal Canadian Air Force?
IT'S OFFICIAL: THE CONSERVATIVE PARTY OF CANADA HAS CHANGED ITS NAME TO THE ROYAL PAIN IN THE ASS PARTY of CANADA
NEWS
AISLIN 11
MONTREAL THE GAZETTE

Stephen Harper loves the Royal Family…

…there having been four Royal visits to Canada in as many years.

A postal strike was resolved during the Royal visit of Prince William and the Duchess of Cambridge.

Proroguery seems to be very much to Stephen Harper's liking.

The decisive federal election of May of 2011…

...saw a relentless series of attack ads directed at Liberal leader Michael Ignatieff...

…that led to the elimination of the Liberal party as the official Opposition.

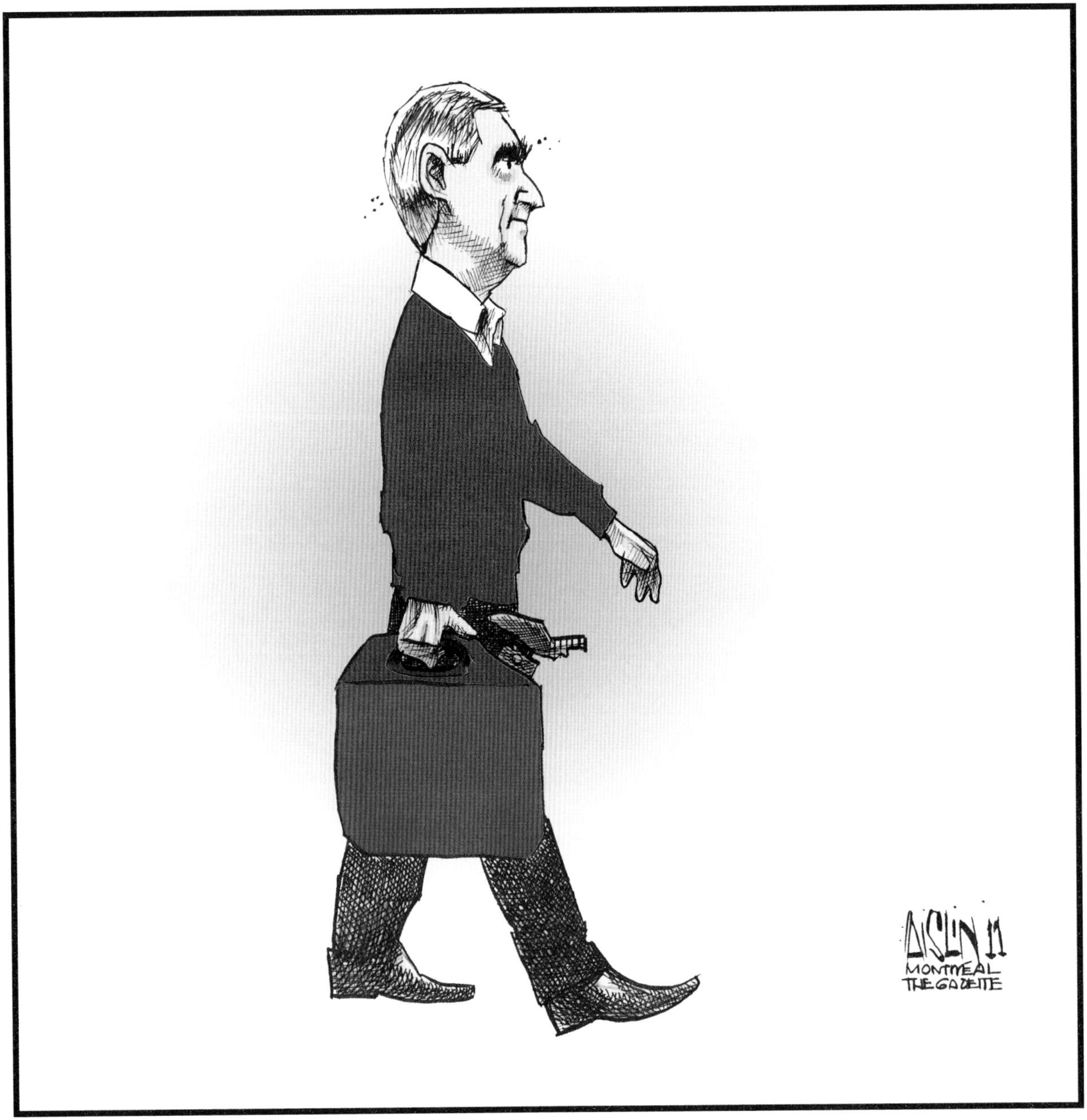
AISLIN 11
MONTREAL
THE GAZETTE

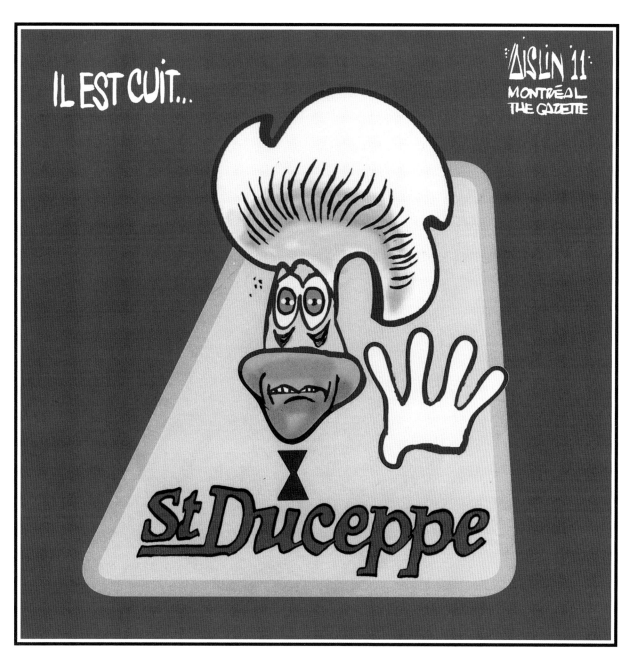

The Bloc Québécois and Gilles Duceppe were reduced to a dismal total of four seats.

Some good news: Elizabeth May, the leader of the Green Party, was elected to Parliament.

Despite failing health, NDP leader Jack Layton had the stamina to carry out the most important election of his political career

That led to an orange wave sweeping across Quebec with the election of 58 seats, and the new role for the NDP as official Opposition.

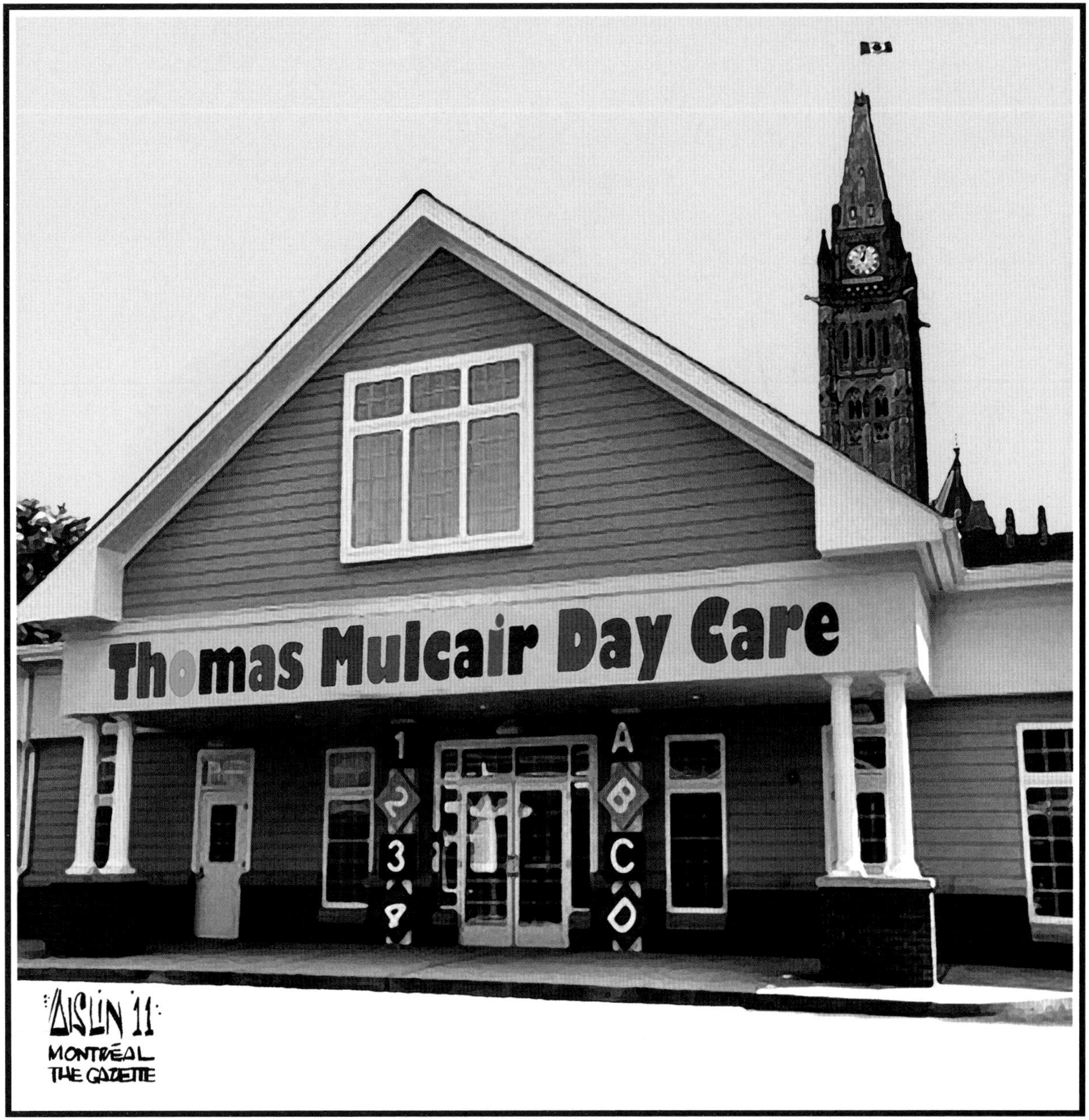
Thomas Mulcair Day Care
1
2
3
4
A
B
C
D
AISLIN '11
MONTRÉAL
THE GAZETTE

Mind you, many of the new Quebec members were some of the youngest, least-experienced caucus members to ever enter the House of Commons.

Members of all political parties mourned the passing of Jack Layton shortly after the federal election.

Layton would be replaced by the scrappy Thomas Mulcair as NDP and Opposition leader.

The election was tainted by scandal with reports of controversial automated, misleading robocalls being made to voters.

Nevertheless, there has been a massive changing of the colours in Ottawa.

Minister of the Environment Peter Kent receives the Fossil Award at climate talks in Durban, South Africa.

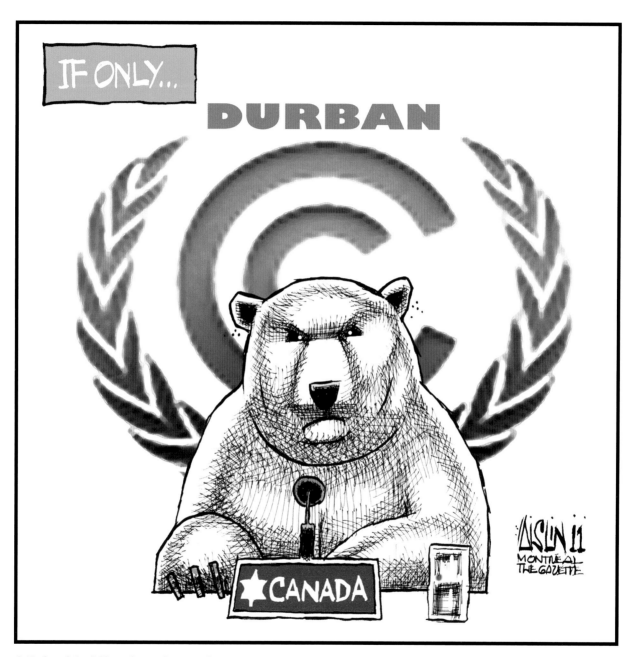

Might this fellow have been a better representative of Canadian concerns?

One of Stephen Harper's main preoccupations is with Canada's north.

Do you think he might build a prison in Nunavut?

Defence Minister Peter MacKay likes to test-run our search-and-rescue helicopters.

Our 2011 Christmas gift wish list included a new heart for Stephen Harper…

...some traction winter tires for Bob Rae...

…and a plunger air-guitar for Justin Trudeau who famously called Environment Minister Peter Kent "a piece of shit" in the House of Commons!

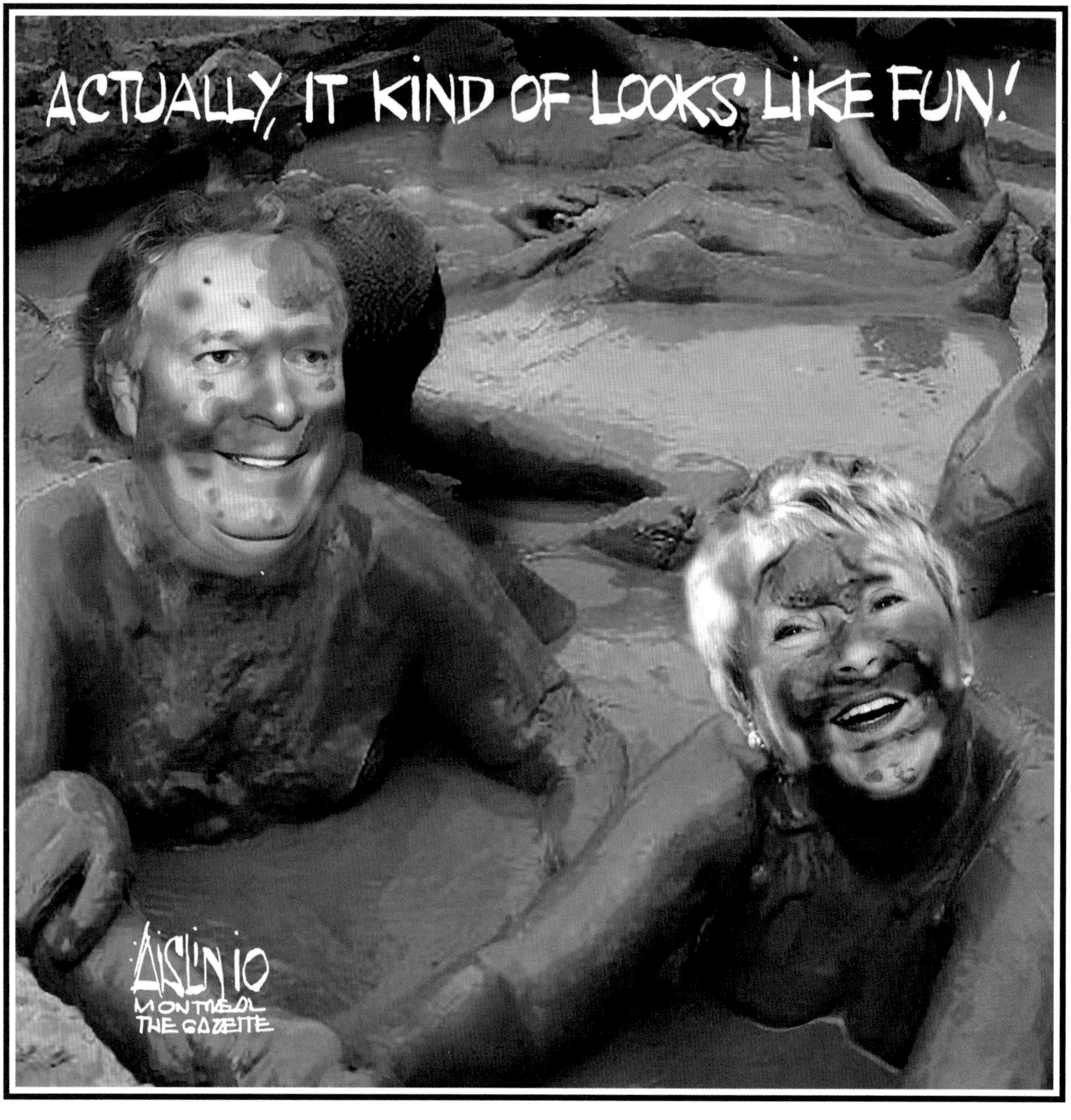
ACTUALLY, IT KIND OF LOOKS LIKE FUN!
AISLIN 10
MONTREAL
THE GAZETTE

As this academic year comes to a close...

Québésport!

All politics in Quebec are games – and all sport in Quebec is political. Understanding this fully, Jean Charest – never the most popular figure in Quebec – has survived three terms as Premier. It's hard to know if he could survive to serve an additional term given the short tempers flaring in Quebec over the recent student demonstrations and allegations of widespread corruption in the construction industry. Newly arrived CAQ leader François Legault and Parti Québécois leader Pauline Marois both want Charest's job. Why anyone would want the job in the first place is a bit of a puzzle, given that it is the most difficult one in Canada. Nevertheless, in the meantime, the English population of Quebec quietly goes about its business, even when being bashed by the Parti Québécois or Le Journal de Montréal. All signs of protest within the community have gone dark or moved on elsewhere.

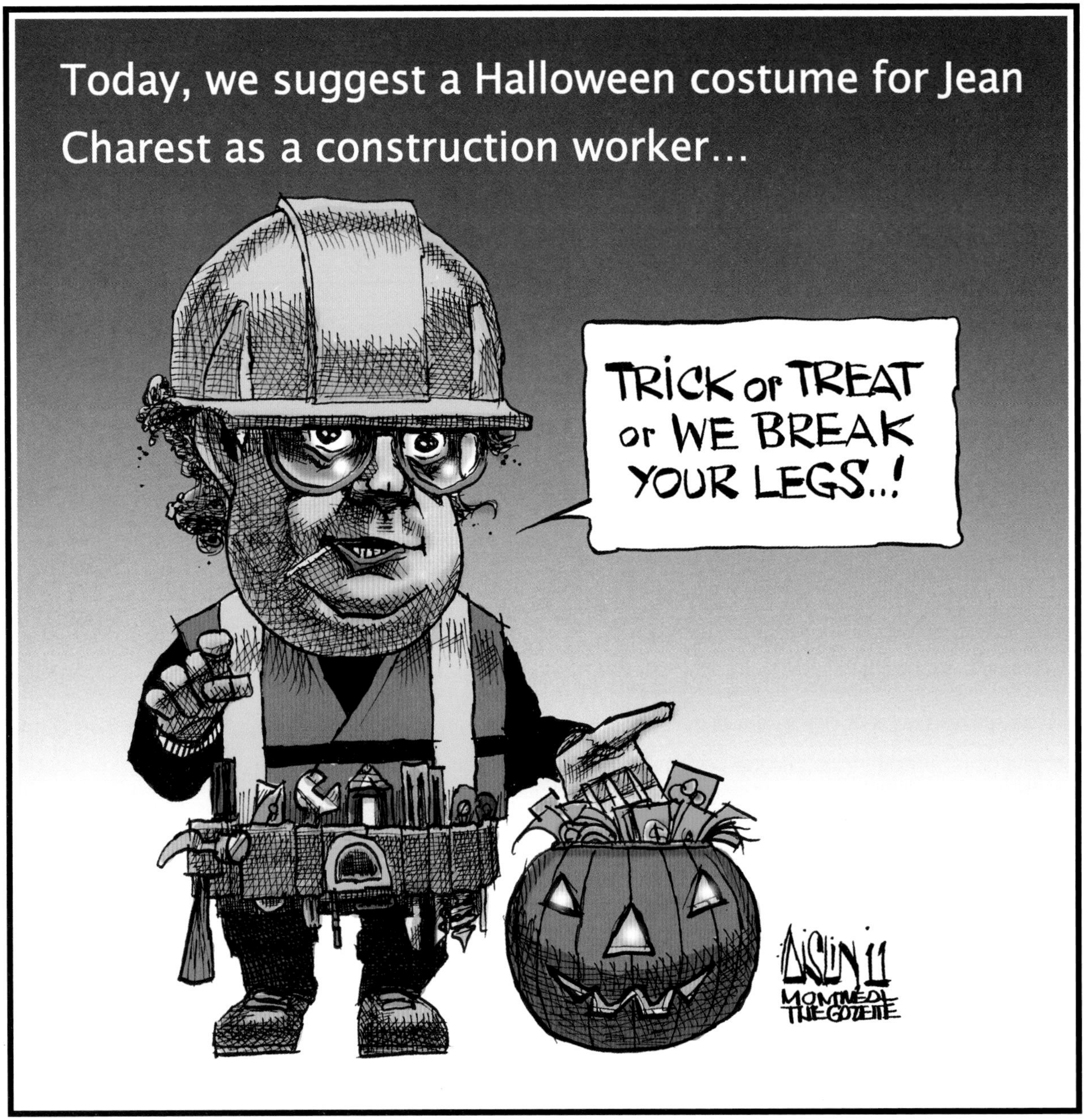
Today, we suggest a Halloween costume for Jean Charest as a construction worker...
TRICK or TREAT or WE BREAK YOUR LEGS..!
AISLIN 11
MONTREAL THE GAZETTE

Corruption here...

Pocketing cash gifts is legal

QUEBEC QUIRK
Politicians can take money, not declare it

LINDA GYULAI
GAZETTE CIVIC AFFAIRS REPORTER

City councillors and provincial MNAs can accept cash gifts of any amount and from any source – so long as they put the money in their pocket and not in their party's coffers.

...AND A MAN'S SUIT HAS 14 POCKETS!

...corruption there...

...corruption, corruption everywhere!

Quebec halts shale gas exploration after protests are heeded.

This is how many Outremont types spend their weekends.

This is how many police types spend their working hours.

How some of the niqab types might actually fit in to our society.

François Legault, the new leader of the Coalition Avenir Québec

Pauline Marois rides again.

A new logo for the rapidly aging Parti Québécois.

Playing the anti-Anglo card.

A huge threat to Quebec culture!

Quebec anglos are a distinct minority: Fraser

MIKE DESOUZA
POSTMEDIA NEWS

OTTAWA – Quebec's anglophones are not in danger of disappearing, but often feel invisible without flexible government programs and policies to support their growth, says Canada's language watchdog.

Graham Fraser, commissioner of official languages, told a Senate committee examining the minority English-speaking population

credentials, had higher rates of poverty and fewer public-sector jobs.

He said recent research by his office has demonstrated that there is a sense of isolation for English-speaking Quebecers who live outside the Montreal region.

"The English la[nguage] in danger." Fras[er] lenge lies in ensu[ring] and vitality of the community in Q[uebec]

AA meeting

Hi... MY NAME IS STAN, and I'm an ANGLOPHONE

AISLIN 10
MONTREAL
THE GAZETTE

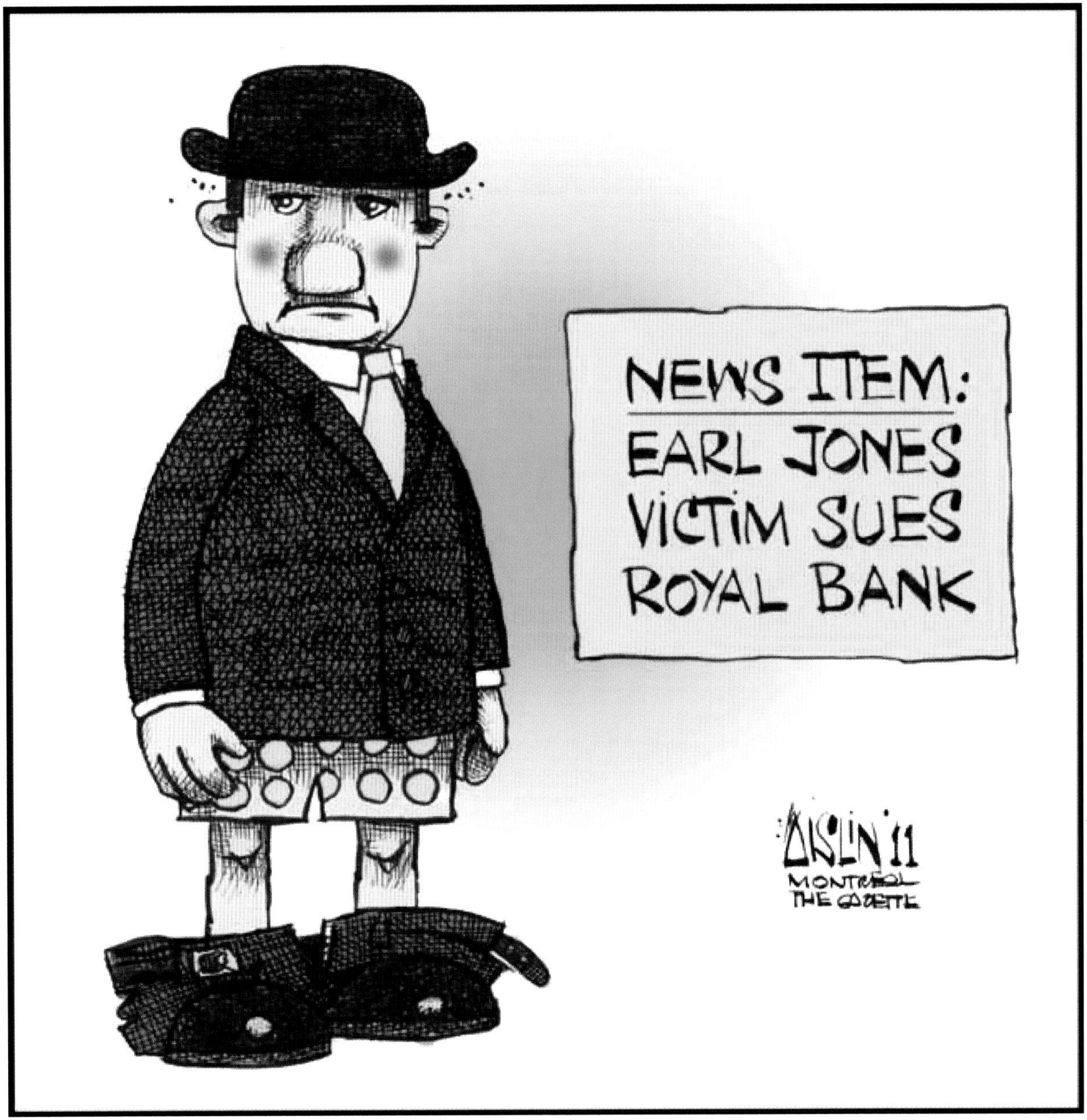
NEWS ITEM:
EARL JONES
VICTIM SUES
ROYAL BANK
AISLIN '11

The Royal Bank, probably embarrassed about its connection with Earl Jones, settles with the shyster's victims by agreeing to pay out $17 million. Unpublished.

Quebec City desperately wants an NHL franchise…

…and an arena to house the team.

In 2010, we all took a break from hockey to watch the World Cup.

Should a new World Cup trophy include Paul – the German oracle octopus?

That same year, we watched the spectacular hockey from the damp winter Olympic Games in Vancouver…

…and then returned to watching the same-old same-old NHL.

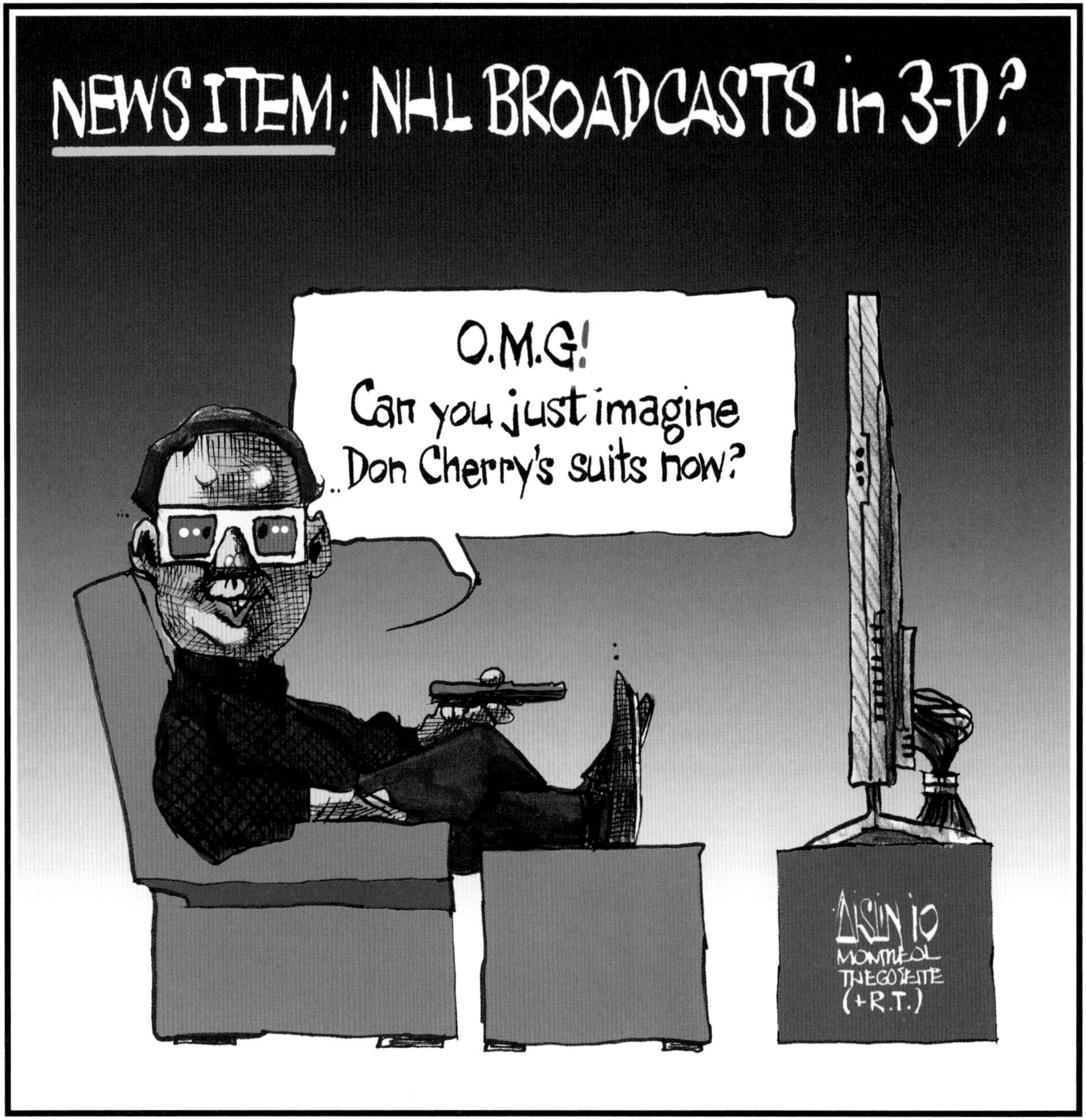
NEWS ITEM: NHL BROADCASTS in 3-D?
O.M.G!
Can you just imagine
..Don Cherry's suits now?
AISLIN 10
MONTREAL
THE GAZETTE
(+R.T.)

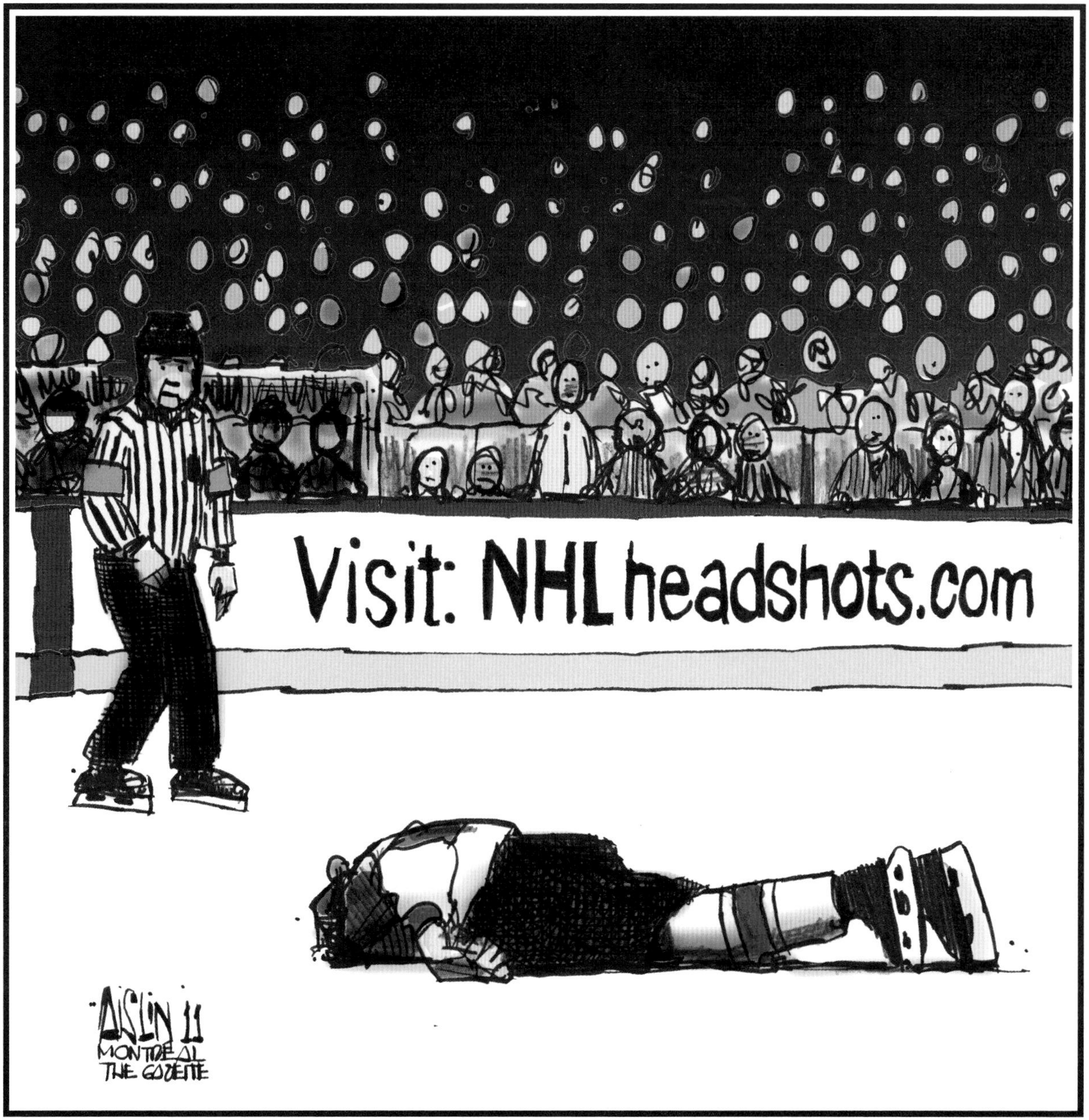
Visit: NHLheadshots.com
AISLIN 11
MONTREAL THE GAZETTE

When the Dalai Lama visited Montreal, instead of giving him some religious relic from one of our many cathedrals, we gave him a Habs jersey.

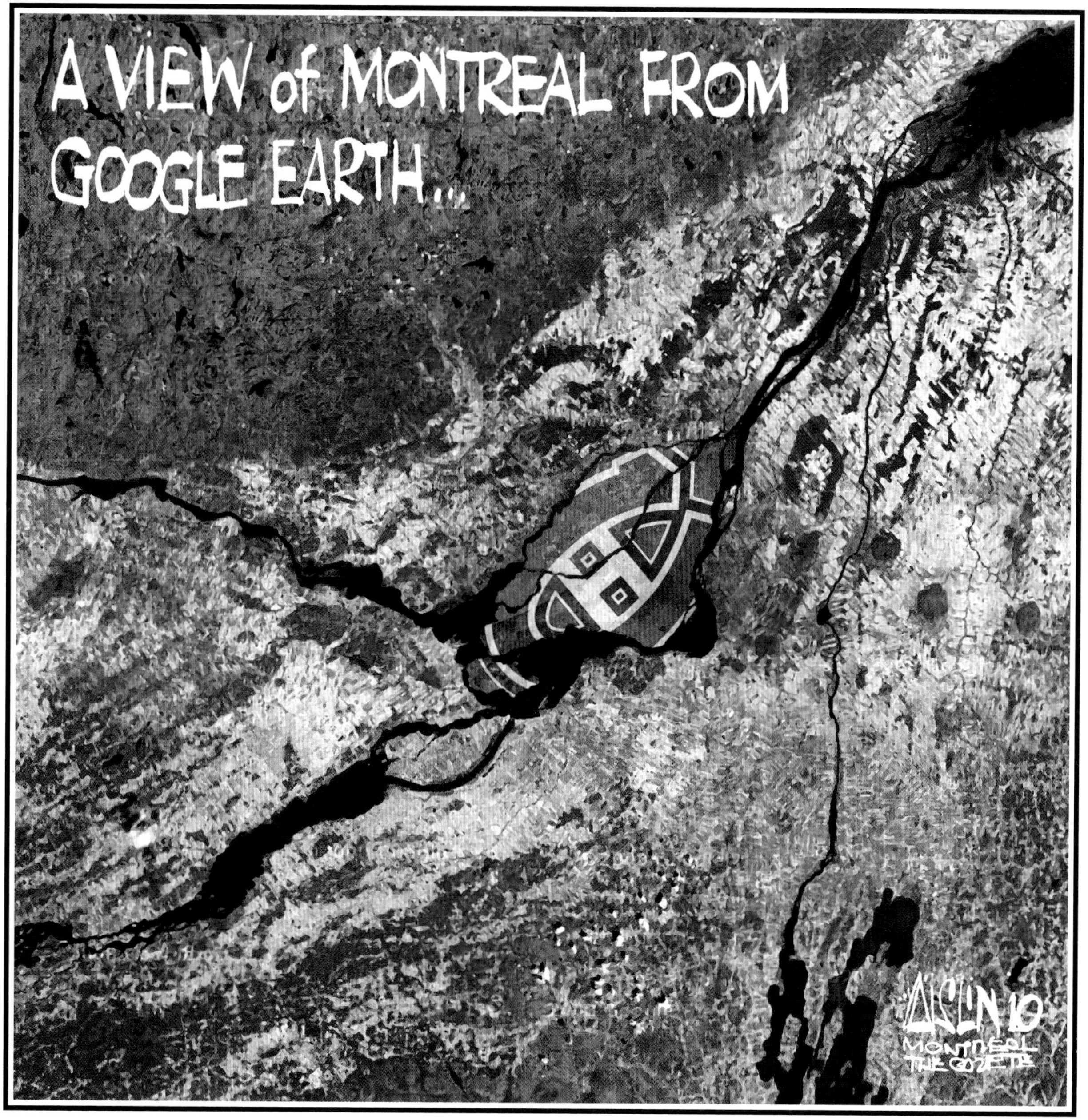
A VIEW of MONTREAL FROM
GOOGLE EARTH...

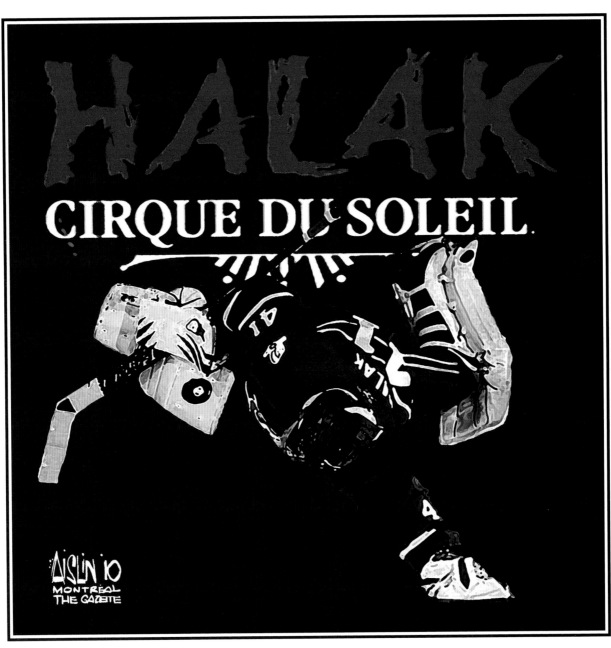

However briefly, the Habs raised our hopes with the spectacular goaltending of Jaroslav Halak during the 2010 playoffs.

Even Pauline Marois became a Canadiens fan.

But then, the Habs traded away Halak…

…and it has been downhill ever since.

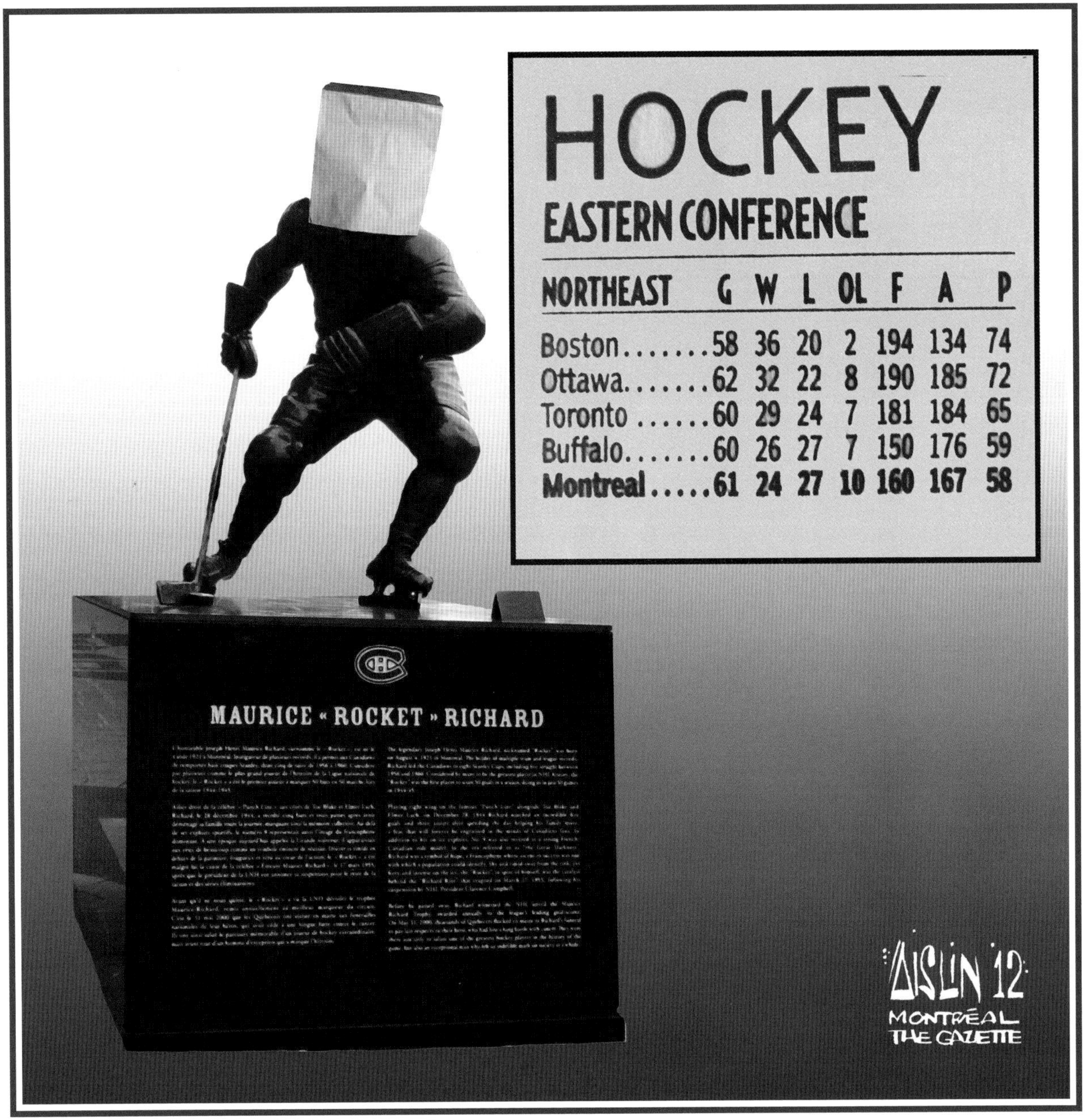
HOCKEY
EASTERN CONFERENCE
NORTHEAST G W L OL F A P
Boston.......58 36 20 2 194 134 74
Ottawa.......62 32 22 8 190 185 72
Toronto 60 29 24 7 181 184 65
Buffalo.......60 26 27 7 150 176 59
Montreal.....61 24 27 10 160 167 58
MAURICE « ROCKET » RICHARD
AISLIN 12
MONTRÉAL
THE GAZETTE

The last game of last season between the two last place teams!

Montréal Caché

So, yes, the current Habs are the worst team in living memory. Student mobs roam our streets at will, demanding that everything be free, leaving the rest of us to pay for it. It's a good thing those kids are walking, too, because, if you drive in Montreal, you just can't get there from here or anywhere else for that matter. Our infrastructure is crumbling, and our bridges are falling down at a faster rate than any other municipality in Canada. Corruption is everywhere, including City Hall. And we're the most heavily taxed people in North America. And yet, and yet…Montreal is still one of the coolest cities to live in: You just have to know where to hide.

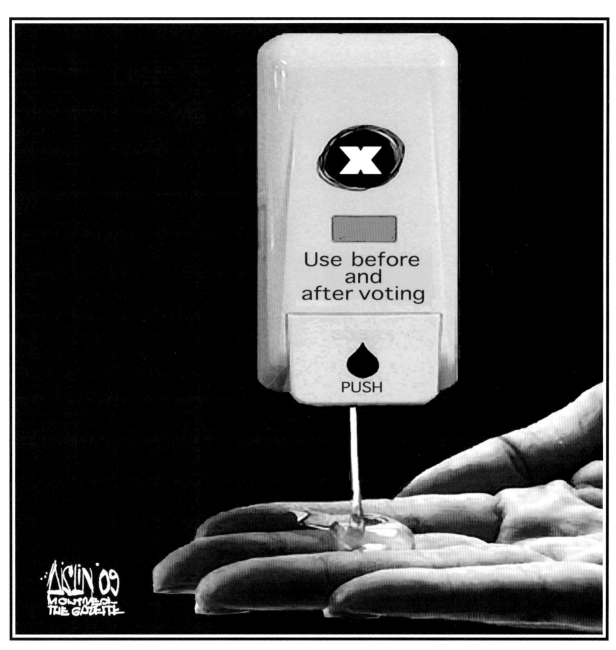

We washed our hands before the last municipal election, but just couldn't decide on who to vote for…

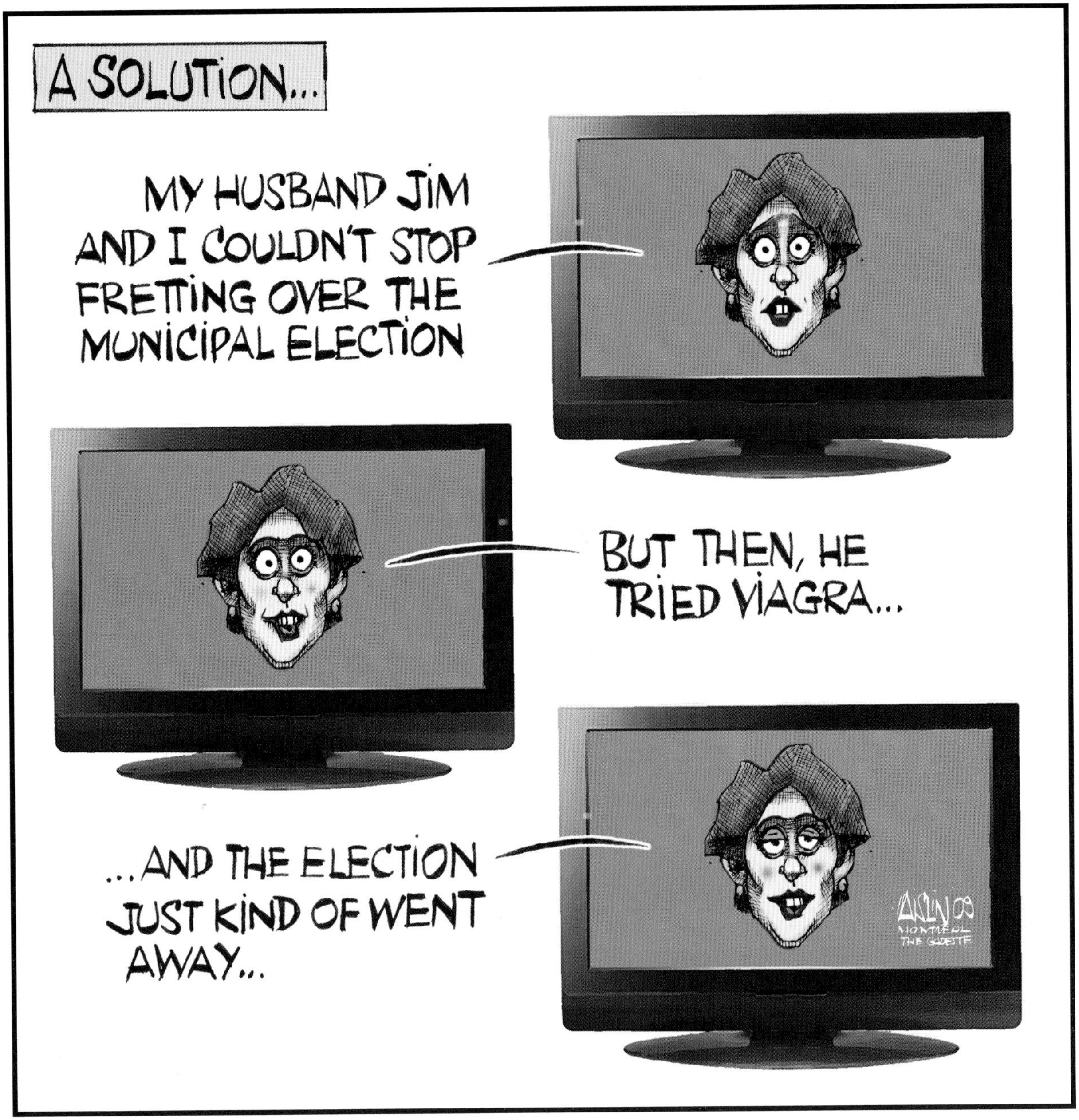
A SOLUTION...
MY HUSBAND JIM AND I COULDN'T STOP FRETTING OVER THE MUNICIPAL ELECTION
BUT THEN, HE TRIED VIAGRA...
...AND THE ELECTION JUST KIND OF WENT AWAY...
AISLIN 09
MONTREAL THE GAZETTE

Would the next mayor be the left-wing separatist, Louise Harel, or the bumbling incumbent, Gérald Tremblay?

The Saint Patrick's Day parade of late.

Montreal mayor, Gérald Tremblay.

A fallen piece of concrete forced the closure of Montreal's busy Ville-Marie tunnel thoroughfare.

Montreal's Champlain Bridge is constantly being closed for repairs.

Montreal's Mercier Bridge is constantly being closed for repairs.

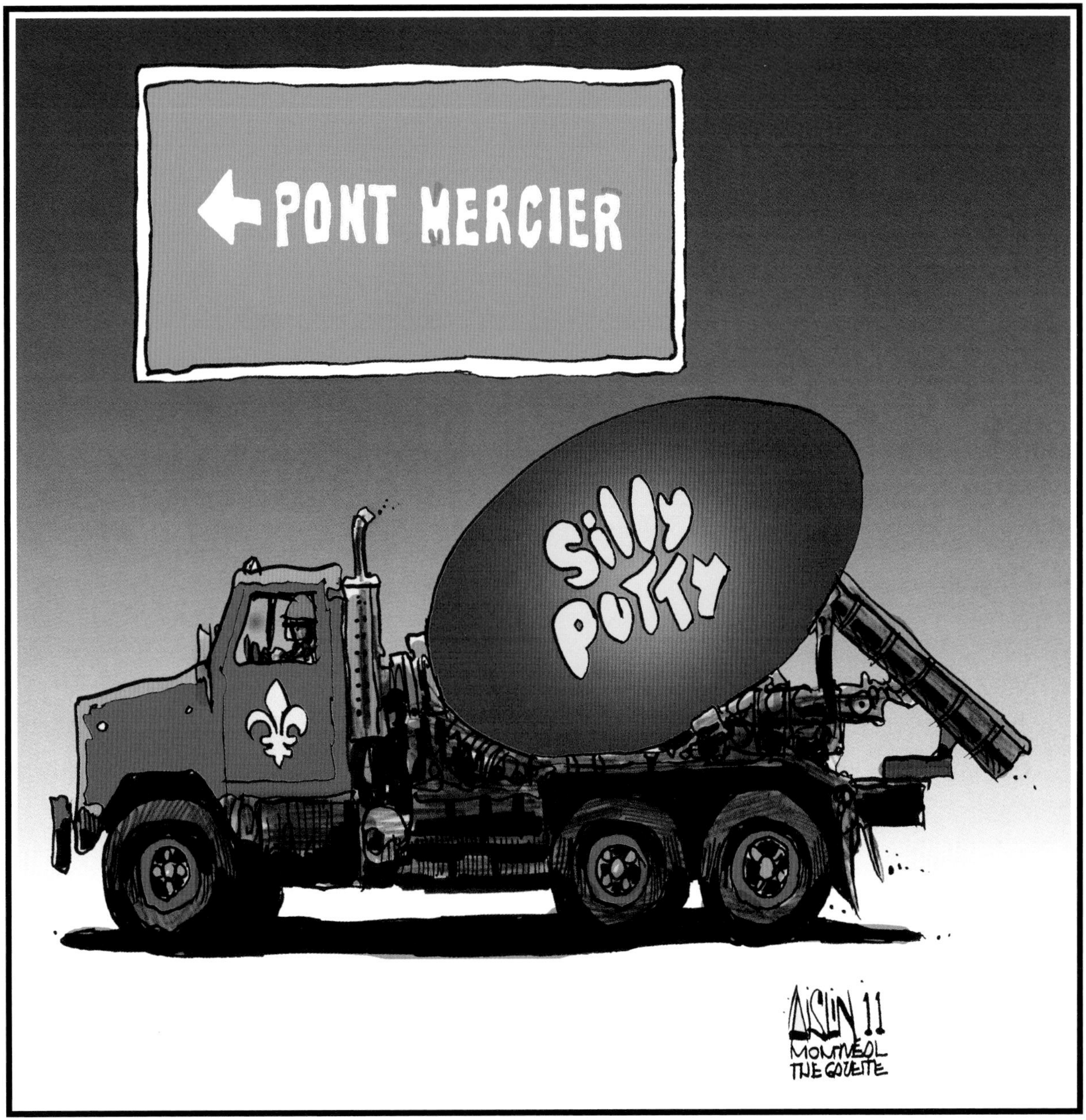

PONT MERCIER
Silly PUTTY
AISLIN 11
MONTREAL THE GAZETTE

Many are happy with the announcement that the Champlain Bridge will be replaced.

Meanwhile, down at City Hall…

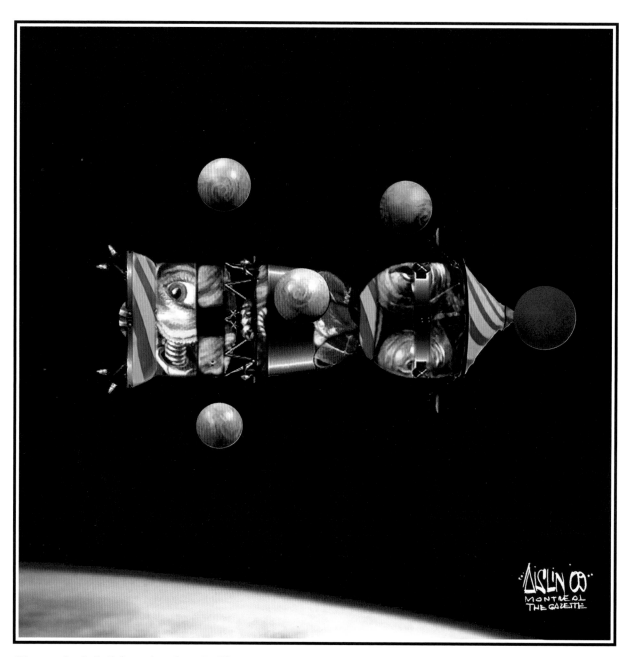

Cirque du Soleil founder Guy Laliberté pays $15 million to fly into space…

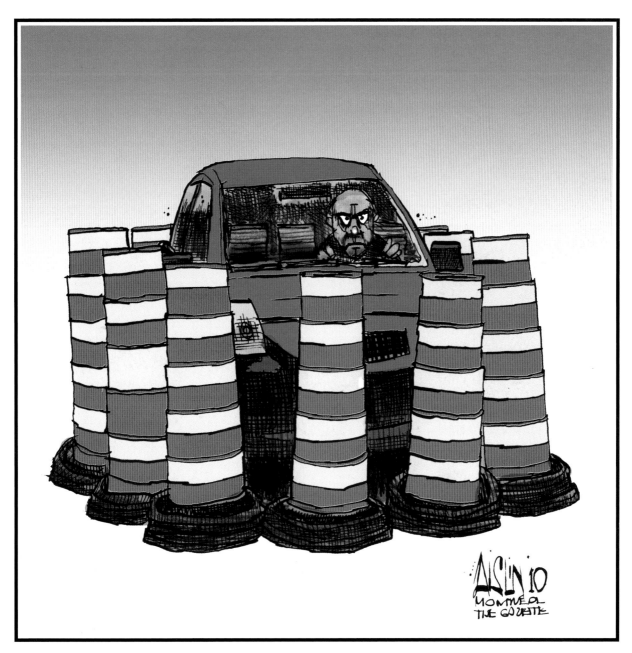

…while your average Montrealer can't get around the block.

Those traffic construction cones are absolutely everywhere!

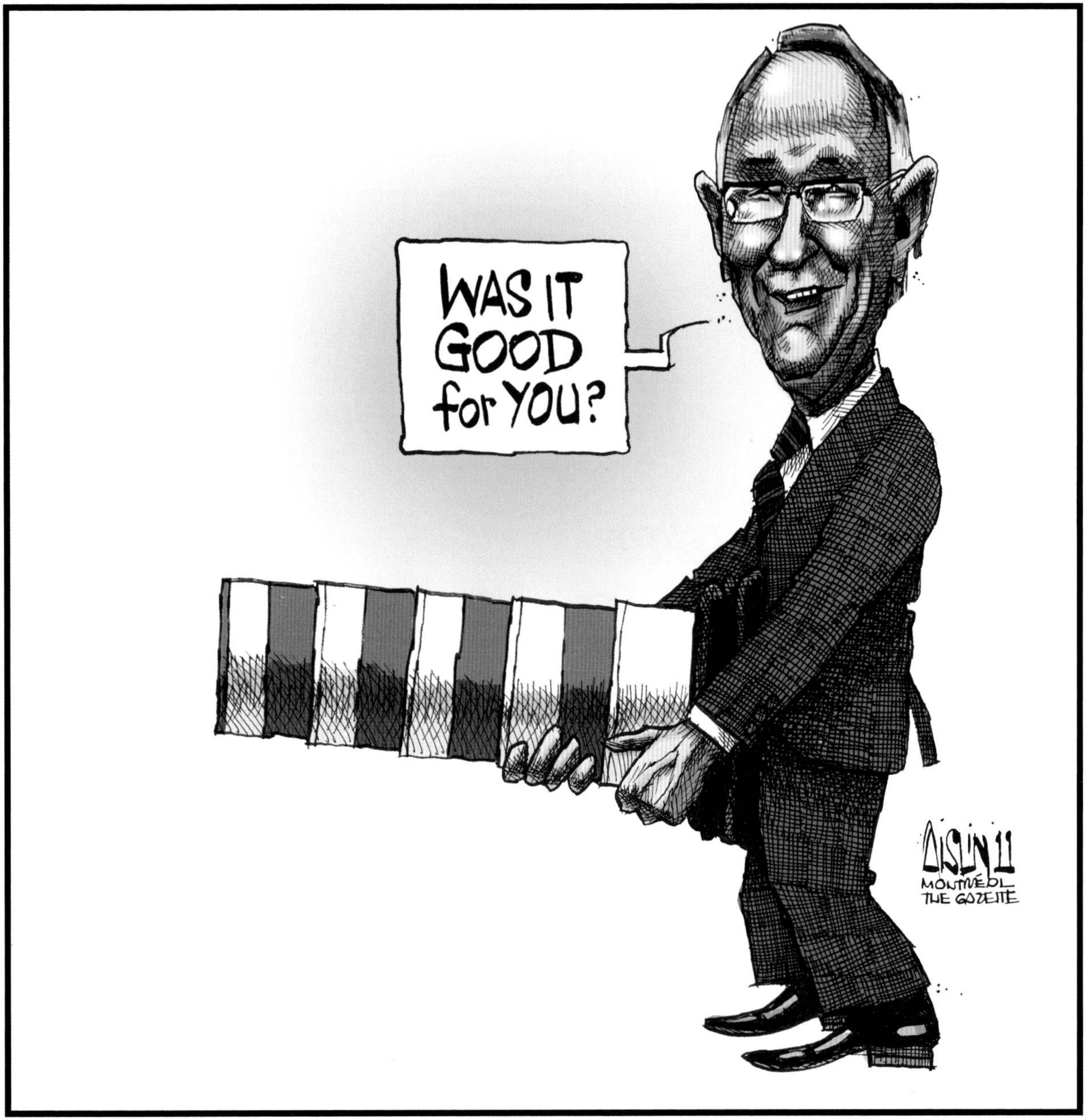
WAS IT GOOD for YOU?
AISLIN 11
MONTREAL THE GAZETTE

AISLIN 10
IN THE SPIRIT OF NASRETTIN HOCA

Hürriyet, Istanbul

AISLIN is the name of Terry Mosher's elder daughter, and the nom de plume he has used for over forty years as the political cartoonist for Montreal's English-language newspaper, *The Gazette*.

In recognition both of his charitable work and his contribution to the world of political cartooning, Mosher was named an Officer of the Order of Canada in May 2003.

Mosher, the most recent president of the Association of Canadian Editorial Cartoonists, often serves as a judge at international cartoon competitions, most recently in Portugal and Turkey. In August of 2012, he will travel to China to address a major cartoon and animation conference that is held there annually.

More information is available at: **www.aislin.com**

Other books by Aislin:

Aislin–100 Caricatures (1971)

Hockey Night in Moscow (1972, with Jack Ludwig)

Aislin–150 Caricatures (1973)

The Great Hockey Thaw (1974, with Jack Ludwig)

'Ello, Morgentaler? Aislin–150 Caricatures (1975)

O.K. Everybody Take a Valium! Aislin–150 Caricatures (1977)

L'Humour d'Aislin (1977)

The Retarded Giant (1977, with Bill Mann)

The Hecklers: A History of Canadian Political Cartooning
   (1979, with Peter Desbarats)

The Year The Expos Almost Won the Pennant
   (1979, with Brodie Snyder)

Did the Earth Move? Aislin–180 Caricatures (1980)

The Year The Expos Finally Won Something
   (1981, with Brodie Snyder)

The First Great Canadian Trivia Quiz
   (1981, with Brodie Snyder)

Stretchmarks (1982)

The Anglo Guide to Survival in Quebec
   (1983, with various Montreal writers)

Tootle: A Children's Story (1984, with Johan Sarrazin)

Where's the Trough? (1985)

Old Whores (1987)

What's the Big Deal? (1988, with Rick Salutin)

The Lawn Jockey (1989)

Parcel of Rogues (1990, with Maude Barlow)

Barbed Lyres, Canadian Venomous Verse
   (1990, with Margaret Atwood and other Canadian poets)

Drawing Bones–15 Years of Cartooning Brian Mulroney (1991)

Put Up & Shut Up! The 90s so far in Cartoons
   (1994, with Hubie Bauch)

Oh, Canadians! Hysterically Historical Rhymes
   (1996, with Gordon Snell)

One Oar in the Water: The Nasty 90s continued in cartoons (1997)

Oh, No! More Canadians! Hysterically Historical Rhymes
   (1998, with Gordon Snell)

Nick: A Montreal Life (1998, with Dave Bist, L. Ian Macdonald,
   Stephen Phizicky)

2000 Reasons to Hate the Millennium
   (1999, with Josh Freed and other contributors)

The Big Wind-Up! The final book of Nasty 90s cartoons (1999)

Yes! Even More Canadians! Hysterically Historical Rhymes
   (2000, with Gordon Snell)

The Oh, Canadians Omnibus (2001, with Gordon Snell)

In Your Face … other recent cartoons (2001)

More Marvellous Canadians! (2002, with Gordon Snell)

The Illustrated Canadian Songbook, (2003, with Bowser & Blue)

Further Fabulous Canadians! (2004, with Gordon Snell)

OH,OH! …and other recent cartoons (2004)

The Best Of OH! CANADIANS (2006, with Gordon Snell)

Mordecai Richler Was Here (2006, with Mordecai Richler)

What Next? …and other recent cartoons by Aislin (2006)

Aislin's Shenanigans …and other recent cartoons by Aislin (2009)

Finn's Thin Book Of Irish Ironies with Patrick Watson (2010)

Polar Lines (2011, with Stephen Hendrie)

Caricature•Cartoon Canada (2012, Terry Mosher, editor)